WHITE BELT
SUDOKU™

Michael Rios

Sterling Publishing Co., Inc.
New York

CONTENTS

8   10   9   7

Martial Arts Sudoku and White Belt Sudoku
are trademarks of Sterling Publishing Co., Inc.

Published by Sterling Publishing Co., Inc.
387 Park Avenue South, New York, NY 10016
© 2005 by Michael Rios
Distributed in Canada by Sterling Publishing
c/o Canadian Manda Group, 165 Dufferin Street,
Toronto, Ontario, Canada M6K 3H6
Distributed in the United Kingdom by GMC Distribution Services,
Castle Place, 166 High Street, Lewes, East Sussex, England BN7 1XU
Distributed in Australia by Capricorn Link (Australia) Pty. Ltd.
P.O. Box 704, Windsor, NSW 2756, Australia

Sterling ISBN-13: 978-1-4027-3595-0
ISBN-10: 1-4027-3595-2

For information about custom editions, special sales, premium and
corporate purchases, please contact Sterling Special Sales
Department at 800-805-5489 or specialsales@sterlingpub.com.

INTRODUCTION

To solve sudoku puzzles, all you need to know is this one simple rule:

Fill in the boxes so that each of the nine rows, each of the nine columns, and each of the nine 3×3 sections contain all the numbers from 1 to 9.

And that's all there is to it! Using these simple rules, let's see how far we get on this sample puzzle at right. (The letters at the top and left edges of the puzzle are for reference only; you won't see them in the regular puzzles.)

	A	B	C	D	E	F	G	H	I
J									
K			2				1	8	4
L	9		5		7		2		6
M	1		4	3	9	2		7	
N				7		6			
O		7		1	4	8	9		2
P	3		2		6		8		5
Q	8	4	9		3				
R									

The first number that can be filled in is an obvious one: box EN is the only blank box in the center 3×3 section, and all the digits 1 through 9 are represented except for 5. EN must be 5.

The next box is a little trickier to discover. Consider the upper left 3×3 section of the puzzle. Where can a 4 go? It can't go in AK, BK, or CK because row K already has a 4 at IK. It can't go in BJ or BL because column B already has a 4 at BQ. It can't go in CJ because column C already has a 4 at CM. So it must go in AJ.

Another box in that same section that can now be filled is BJ. A 2 can't go in AK, BK, or CK due to the 2 at EK. The 2 at GL rules out a 2 at BL. And the 2 at CP means that a 2 can't go in CJ. So BJ must contain the 2. It is worth noting that this 2 couldn't have been placed without the 4 at AJ in place. Many of the puzzles rely on this type of steppingstone behavior.

We now have a grid as shown.

Let's examine column A. There are four blank boxes in column A; in which blank box must the 2 be placed? It can't be AK because of the 2 in EK (and the 2 in BJ). It can't be AO because of the 2 in IO. It can't be AR because of the 2 in CP. Thus, it must be AN that has the 2.

	A	B	C	D	E	F	G	H	I
J	4	2							
K					2		1	8	4
L	9		5		7		2		6
M	1		4	3	9	2		7	
N				7	5	6			
O		7		1	4	8	9		2
P	3		2		6		8		5
Q	8	4	9		3				
R									

By the 9's in AL, EM, and CQ, box BN must be 9. Do you see how?

We can now determine the value for box IM. Looking at row M and then column I, we find all the digits 1 through 9 are represented but 8. IM must be 8.

This brief example of some of the techniques leaves us with the grid at right.

You should now be able to use what you learned to fill in CN followed by BL, then HL followed by DL and FL.

As you keep going through this puzzle, you'll find it gets easier as you fill in more. And as you keep working through the puzzles in this book, you'll find it gets easier and more fun each time. The final answer is shown below.

	A	B	C	D	E	F	G	H	I
J	4	2							
K					2		1	8	4
L	9		5		7		2		6
M	1		4	3	9	2		7	8
N	2	9		7	5	6			
O		7		1	4	8	9		2
P	3		2		6		8		5
Q	8	4	9		3				
R									

This book consists of 300 puzzles of easy level of difficulty.

—Michael Rios

	A	B	C	D	E	F	G	H	I
J	4	2	1	6	8	3	5	9	7
K	7	3	6	5	2	9	1	8	4
L	9	8	5	4	7	1	2	3	6
M	1	5	4	3	9	2	6	7	8
N	2	9	8	7	5	6	4	1	3
O	6	7	3	1	4	8	9	5	2
P	3	1	2	9	6	7	8	4	5
Q	8	4	9	2	3	5	7	6	1
R	5	6	7	8	1	4	3	2	9

1

2				4	1	6	5	
			9	6	3		1	
	1						9	
							8	4
9	4						7	6
8	6							
	2						4	
	7		4	5	6			
	8	1	7	9				3

2

4	9		6					
8	7				9			5
						6	2	
	2		8	6		5	3	4
6	4	3		7	2		9	
	8	7						
5			7				8	6
					8		5	1

3

8	7			6				
			8	5			7	
	1	4			2	9		
9				4				2
2	4						1	7
1				8				5
		9	6			3	8	
	8			3	5			
				1			5	9

4

	6		5	4			2	
		7				4		
4			8			6		
3	9	1		8				2
2								3
7				9		1	4	8
		9			6			1
		5				3		
	7			3	8		5	

5

5		3			1	4		
	2		5					9
		8		2		7		
		2		6		8	4	
8		7				6		2
	6	4		8		5		
		6		1		9		
4					7		6	
		5	6			2		7

6

	4		1	5		9	8	
2			6					
	8	5						
6	2			8	5			
8	9						3	5
			9	4			2	6
						6	5	
					1			7
	6	8		2	7		9	

3				2		7	1	
	4					9		
		1		9	7			2
		7			5		2	
		5	8	7	1	3		
	3		2			1		
8			6	4		2		
		3					9	
	2	4		1				8

	2	4			1	5		9
		1		9	4			
	7		8			1		
			9					
	8	9	4	3	5	7	2	
					8			
		7			3		6	
			5	2		3		
5		2	7			8	9	

Puzzle 9

5			9				3	
8		3			2	7		
				5		2		8
	3			8		5		2
			2		4			
7		4		1			9	
4		9		3				
		5	6			9		3
	7				9			5

Puzzle 10

					9	2	6	
			7		6			
4		9		2		1		7
6		7					5	9
		4				3		
5	3					7		1
2		8		6		5		3
			9		1			
	7	5	8					

				4	9	1	3	
	3							5
4		7	3				8	
5				8		6	9	
6								3
	9	4		7				8
	1				4	8		6
8							5	
	5	3	9	6				

8				5		7	9	
	7				2	3		
9		2	1			6		5
2	6		3					
					1		2	6
6		1			7	5		8
		5	2				3	
	8	9		1				7

1 / 3

		7		4				
6	8	3		9		7		
	9	2	7	5				3
			4					
	7	4		1		2	3	
					3			
1				3	4	9	7	
		5		6		3	1	4
				2		8		

1 / 4

			1				2	
		1		7		3	5	9
		7			9			1
		6	7		1	9		8
				5				
7		3	2		8	1		
8			3			5		
1	7	4		8		6		
	3				2			

1 / 5

	2	7			4		1	6
				7			3	8
				2				
	9	5			6	3		
7			2		5			1
		1	7			6	4	
				3				
9	7			1				
5	3		4			1	7	

1 / 6

	5				9		1	
				5		4	2	9
6		9		1		5		
	6					9		7
	1			4			3	
3		5					8	
		8		9		3		5
1	3	6		8				
	9		7				4	

3				1				8	
			4	3				
7	4				8			3
	2	7						4
5	1	6				8	2	7
4						6	1	
6			3				5	8
				6	1			
	8			7				2

				5			3	
1				8	2	7	9	
						1		8
	6	9	5			3		
		5	7		3	6		
		7			9	2	8	
5		6						
	3	4	2	9				7
	2			6				

3		2	8					5
		6				1		
			2	4		3		
7		1			2		6	9
			6		9			
8	6		1			5		7
		7		5	6			
		3				7		
9					7	6		3

	4	1		8		6		
	5				3		4	8
	7							
	2	4	3	1				
		7	5		2	4		
				7	8	5	6	
							7	
9	6		2				3	
		8		3		2	5	

2 / 1

2	4				7			6
	1						8	
			2	5	9	1		
	2	6		7	3			
	9	5				4	6	
			9	4		2	7	
		2	3	8	5			
	5						3	
9			4				2	8

2 / 2

			1	5	3	6		
6	4				7	1	3	
3								8
		6					5	
	3		2	6	5		8	
	7					4		
1								4
	2	4	9				6	7
		9	5	4	8			

2 / 3

		4	9	2	1	5		
		5			8			1
2					4	7		
6			2			9		
4			6		7			8
		8			5			6
		7	1					2
5			8			6		
		6	3	5	2	8		

2 / 4

			4		1	3	8	
8				6				1
	1						9	
1	5		9					3
9		4	1		2	8		6
7					6		1	4
	8						6	
2				9				8
	9	1	7		5			

2 / 5

			2		1	8	3	
								1
2		3	5					
	8	2		5		1		
1	6		3		4		7	8
		5		6		4	9	
					5	3		7
5								
	3	8	6		7			

2 / 6

			5				3	
7		3		1	9			5
8					7		6	
4	9		2		8		7	
			9		1			
	1		7		4		9	8
	7		6					2
5			1	4		7		9
	2				3			

				1			7	
8					6	1		2
			5	4			9	8
		4	7			9	6	
7			1		5			3
	9	3			4	5		
6	1			5	9			
5		2	4					9
	3			8				

	9	5						8
6	1		9		2		5	
		3	5	6				9
9			6				2	
	8						4	
	2				9			7
1				2	6	4		
	3		1		5		6	2
8						1	7	

		7				9	5	
	5	2	6	4				
9	6							
6	2	1	4				8	
3								5
	8				3	4	9	2
							7	9
				2	6	8	4	
	1	8				2		

8	4	7					3	
	6			1	8			
				7		2	8	
				5	6		4	
	9	2				5	1	
	8		2	3				
	7	4		9				
			7	8			5	
	3					7	6	9

Puzzle 3/1

2	4			6		9		
	6	9		8	3		4	
		3						7
9		7						
		6	2		9	5		
						7		9
3						2		
	5		4	9		8	7	
		1		2			9	5

Puzzle 3/2

					9		8	
3	1		6	8				
	9	7		3	5			
		2			6	3	5	
1	7						6	2
	5	3	8			1		
			5	2		4	7	
				7	3		9	1
	4		9					

Puzzle 3/3:

	1	5		7				4
	7		2		6		3	
		6	4			5		
	8		6			2		
1	6						4	7
		2			7		5	
		3			2	4		
	2		1		5		6	
6				4		9	8	

Puzzle 3/4:

1			9			2		
4	7				5			
	3		1	7		5	8	
		7			3			
5	6			8			3	1
			4			6		
	1	5		9	6		4	
			5				1	6
		4			1			9

Puzzle 1:

	3					9		5
		1	3		9		4	
9			8					
		5		7				8
6		7	4		8	3		2
4				3		5		
					2			7
	5		6		7	2		
7		2					9	

Puzzle 2:

9			3				6	5
		1		6				
	3		2	5	7	1		9
		7					5	
5			9		3			2
	6					9		
7		5	8	9	1		3	
				3		5		
3	2				5			7

	8			9		3		
9			8		6	5	1	
		7	3	1				
7		6			8			
	2			4			7	
			1			6		3
				7	3	1		
	7	8	5		2			9
		9		8			5	

1				9				
9				2	5	6	3	1
					3	7		
		6			7			8
	5	1				2	4	
4			5			9		
		4	8					
2	3	8	9	5				6
				6				2

Puzzle 39:

		9				7		
8								3
	5			8		2	1	9
4		7			6		5	
	8		9		1		3	
	9		4			6		7
9	6	1		4			2	
7								6
		8				3		

Puzzle 40:

3								
		4			2		8	1
		8		4		9	7	
	8				6	4	3	
9	6		4		8		1	7
	4	3	7				6	
	1	9		5		7		
2	3		1			6		
								5

4/1

3		4		8				
		6		5	2			
						2		9
7			8	2				5
2	3	5				7	1	8
9				1	7			4
4		3						
			3	6		1		
			7			4		3

4/2

1			6			8		
		6		9	3	2	1	
	2			7	1		5	
		7						
	3		1		6		7	
						6		
	8		7	6			4	
	4	5	3	8		9		
		9			4			3

	7		8					4
	8		7			5	1	
		4		3				7
7					3	2		6
	4						9	
2		6	9					5
9				7		8		
	3	1			6		2	
8					9		6	

		3						6
2		9	1	6		7		3
7					9			
		8					6	7
4	6		5		1		3	8
3	7					2		
			2					5
1		5		9	3	4		2
6						3		

	6	5	9		3			4
	4		7	1				
		3	5			9		
3						8	5	
5				6				3
	8	7						9
		4			2	1		
				8	4		7	
6			3		9	5	4	

	7				5	9	4	1
			8			7	6	
3				4				8
		1			8	3		
		5		1		8		
		9	4			2		
1				2				9
	5	7			4			
9	2	8	1				5	

			8			6		
	5		4				7	1
	1			9	7	4	8	
		6		5			9	
5	4						6	7
	9			6		5		
	7	5	3	4			2	
1	8				9		5	
		2			1			

				9	4	2	6	
	7						8	4
		8			6			1
	4			8	9		3	
			1		3			
	1		7	4			9	
1			9			5		
3	5						2	
		2	4	6	3			

7	2		6					
			7		8	9		6
		3						
	3	2	4	6		1		
		7	8		1	5		
		6		5	9	7	4	
						4		
3		5	9		2			
					4		2	1

	3		7	9	5		1	
7				4				8
					3	9	5	
2	6	7						
4			5		7			2
						6	7	1
	7	8	9					
6				5				9
	4		8	7	6		2	

5
1

Puzzle 5-1:

9	1					2		
			2	1			6	
		8	9	5				
	2			9	4		3	
	4		1		8		2	
	8		3	2			1	
				6	9	4		
	5			3	1			
		7					8	6

5
2

Puzzle 5-2:

8		4					1	
7				9	6			
9	6			4	3			
2		9	4				5	
	1			3			2	
	4				2	9		7
			7	5			6	3
			6	2				8
	7					2		5

Puzzle 53

					4			
		9			2	1		3
1	8	2		6				7
				1			5	
9		8	5		6	2		4
	3			4				
8				2		6	9	5
4		5	3			8		
			6					

Puzzle 54

	6		4	3	8			7
7		4		2		6		
		5	9					
4	8							5
		3				8		
9							3	2
					9	2		
		7		1		3		4
3			7	5	6		9	

			1	4			6	
			3	9				4
		9	6		2	1		
						9	5	
9	6	4		7		8	2	1
	5	2						
		1	4		6	3		
7			5	9				
	9			1	3			

				7				
	5		2	4	3	9		7
	9	6	1		8			
4		2						
	8	9				6	1	
						2		5
			9		5	4	2	
2		3	7	6	4		9	
				3				

	6			5			8	
3		7			8			
				1	7		2	4
5		2					7	8
		4				6		
9	7					4		2
4	5		1	3				
			7			8		3
	2			9			4	

	2	1		8	6		4	
		3		1	2	8		
			9					
4			5	7				1
		9				4		
2				4	9			6
					4			
		6	3	5		1		
	4		2	6		3	7	

						6		1
5	3				4		7	2
7		6						
	4		7	5			1	
		9	4		1	7		
	2		3	6			5	
						8		4
2	1		8				3	7
8		3						

		2	3	1	9	7		4
4							3	
		3			2	6		
				6	5			
	8	9	1		3	5	4	
			9	4				
		8	7			1		
	2							9
9		6	2	5	8	4		

6/1

			7	9	4	8		
			5					3
	8					4	7	6
3		4				1	6	
8				2				9
	9	1				7		2
1	5	8					9	
7					6			
		2	9	8	1			

6/2

6			9				5	2
			7			8	6	
	7					9		1
2		3	8	1		6	9	
	1	9		3	6	4		7
4		5					1	
	2	1			9			
9	6				5			4

Puzzle 6-3

		8	3	9			7	
					5	4		8
2	5	9			4			
				3		2		1
		5	1		2	7		
3		2		7				
			9			6	4	7
5		7	6					
	3			2	7	8		

Puzzle 6-4

2				6			7	
			9	8				
	5				2	1	3	
	1	4	2	5				8
		7				2		
8				9	4	3	1	
	7	6	4				9	
				7	9			
	8			3				4

6/5

		4	1	5	6		2	
	7							1
	9		2			6		3
					7		3	4
4								8
7	1		3					
8		3			1		9	
1							7	
	2		6	3	4	1		

6/6

	5				3		6	
3			9	6	5			
6			1				3	
		4		1		3		7
5	6						2	4
7		8		2		6		
	4				7			3
			6	3	4			8
	2		8				7	

	2	4	5					
	3			1	8	4		
	9			2				
5			4		2		8	
	6	7				3	2	
	8		3		7			1
				7			5	
		2	8	9			3	
					1	2	9	

1	3				5		2	
6	8	4		2				
		7			6			
4	7				1			2
3								4
2			6				9	3
			2			7		
				9		4	6	5
	4		5				1	9

6			4	2				1
		4		3		6	2	5
						7		
	8	1	2					
		2	1		6	5		
					9	1	8	
		7						
8	2	6		7		9		
9				6	2			4

				9				2
		6			3		7	8
		8	2			5	4	
5	6		4			1		
		9				4		
		7			8		5	6
	3	4			6	8		
9	7		5			6		
6				1				

7 / 1

	9	3	1		7	5		
7		1			3	2		
	4		5					3
	2						1	9
1	8						4	
2					1		6	
		8	9			7		1
		7	3		8	9	2	

7 / 2

							8	3
5	3	9		8		2	1	4
		8						5
2	7		1					
			7	6	5			
					4		3	9
9						4		
3	4	5			1		8	9	7
6	2							

7 / 3

				1	2		9	4
				7	4	8		1
	1		6				5	
							8	2
6			4		5			3
3	9							
	4				8		3	
7		2	9	4				
9	8		2	6				

7 / 4

6						1		9
3			4	6		2		
		4	9		5		7	
		6	1	5				
2			6		4			1
				8	2	4		
	1		2		3	5		
		3		9	8			2
5		2						4

7
5

		3		8				
		8		5	7		4	
5	6					1		
1		6			8		3	7
3								1
7	2		1			9		6
		9					5	2
	3		2	6		8		
				7		6		

7
6

7					2		5	
2				5			9	6
	3		9					2
8			4	1	7	2		
		6	5	8	3			4
9					5		1	
6	8			3				9
	4		2					7

77

		3	5	2	4	1		
						3		
	9	6	3					5
1				6			4	
5			2		8			7
	7			9				2
9					7	4	3	
		7						
		1	4	3	9	2		

78

	4	5	1		9	7		
			2	7				6
6		1	3			5		
				8				5
		3				6		
5			7					
		7			3	9		1
9				2	1			
		2	5		7	4	6	

8					4	1		6
			6	1				
3			9				2	
9	3			6			4	
		1	3	2	9	8		
	5			7			1	9
	4				6			1
				4	2			
2		9	1					8

	1			5			7	
	7	3	8			6		
			3			2	9	
		4	1	7		9		6
			6		4			
1		8		3	5	4		
	3	7			8			
		2			3	8	4	
	8			9			3	

						5	2	6
8		1			3			7
2	6		7		9			1
		8		4	7			3
4			8	3		6		
5			3		8		7	2
1			9			3		4
3	9	7						

		7	2	1	9	8		
		6			4			
			7				1	2
	3	2	8	4		1		
	9						7	
		1		6	5	2	8	
5	1				8			
			3			9		
		9	6	7	1	3		

	9				1		3	
			2					4
3	5		4	6		8	7	
		9						8
7			8	1	3			9
5						4		
	3	8		7	5		9	6
9					2			
	2		3				8	

		2	3					
					2		1	6
7	8	6						
	9			2	4		7	8
	4		6		7		3	
6	5		8	3			2	
						3	8	5
8	7		1					
					9	1		

		9				2	8	
	7			6	5			9
4						7		1
				2	8	1		7
			6		3			
8		1	7	9				
5		2						3
7			3	8			9	
	9	4				8		

	6		7				9	1
1		2		9	6		3	
		9	3					
9		7		2				
8								9
				7		4		5
					5	3		
	9		6	3		8		4
3	4				1		5	

		5			4		7	1
			2	1			9	
				5				4
		4	7	2			3	6
7			5		8			2
2	8			4	9	7		
1				7				
	5			3	2			
4	3		8			1		

								1
6					8	2		7
		2			7		4	9
	5		3			1		8
	7		6		1		5	
8		1			4		7	
1	6		7			9		
9		3	5					4
5								

		3	9	5				
			2				4	
	1	2			3	9		
	6	7		9	1	2		
	2						1	
		9	3	8		5	7	
		5	6			7	9	
	9				8			
				3	9	8		

	2			5	6	4	1	8
			4		1			
	3			8			6	
5							3	
	1		7		2		5	
	8							1
	4			6			2	
			9		4			
9	5	2	8	3			4	

	4	5	6					1
6				4				8
2	9					7		
		8	3	1			9	5
				5				
5	7			9	6	8		
		9					2	3
1				6				9
3					9	5	7	

	4							
		5	4		6	9	8	7
7					9			4
			2	6				8
	3		1		7		2	
2				8	4			
9			5					2
4	2	6	9		3	8		
							4	

7					3	8			6	2
8		2				4				
		3		7		6			8	
	4	8								
				6		7				
								1	3	
	2			9		3		6		
				4				5		1
5	9			8	6					7

	4			5					2	
	6			8					4	
2								1		3
	9	6				2		8		
		1		6		4		2		
		2		3				6	9	
9		3								7
	8					5			1	
	2					1			6	

	3			6		8		1
		7			3	9		
		1		8			3	5
	4		6			7		
9								4
		6			8		9	
1	7			2		4		
		4	8			5		
2		3		9			8	

	9	2		7		4	1	
4	5			1	8		6	
	6							
6	3					2		
			7	8	4			
		5					9	1
							3	
	1		6	3			2	8
	8	9		5		6	7	

1	9				4	6		
	6	3	8		7			
						3		9
3			9			2	6	
		6				1		
	4	2			5			3
8		1						
			7			3	5	1
		7	6				2	8

		3	9		8			1
7	4	8	3				9	
	6	2		4		1		
	7	1		8		4	3	
		9		1		6	8	
	8				5	9	2	7
9			4		6	8		

		7	6					
			8	9		3	1	
8				3				6
	4	8	2					3
3		1				4		9
7					1	2	6	
5				7				1
	9	6		2	4			
					8	9		

1		2			4		7	8
			2					
4		5		9	1			
6		4						3
	9	1				4	6	
7						8		1
			1	8		3		7
					5			
2	1		3			5		6

	4	1			3			9
		5		7				4
		3				7	8	
1	7			3	5			
			1		8			
			2	9			1	6
	1	9				2		
2				1		9		
6			7			3	4	

5	1				2			
	7				6		3	5
		8					1	
		5	3		7	4		
	3	2	6		4	1	5	
		6	5		1	9		
	4					5		
3	2		4				9	
			2				4	6

	1		4		3	2		
9		7				4	8	
		2			5		6	
			1	8	5			4
		1				8		
2		8	6	7				
	2		8			9		
	9	5				6		2
		4	5		9		3	

2			3	9	7			
5				4				
		3	8				9	
	3	6	7	8		1		5
8		4		5	6	7	3	
	5				8	4		
				2				3
			4	3	9			6

		1				8	6	
2		8	7			5		4
				8	6		2	
			6	9	3			
		4				3		
			8	5	4			
	8		5	4				
4		5			9	2		7
	7	9				6		

	2		3		4			8
		8	9	7				
	3	6		8		7		
	1			6		9		
			7		1			
		3		2			1	
		9		1		2	4	
				4	9	8		
1			6		8		7	

					6		2	9
	5	4			8		6	
	6		1	4				
	4			7	1			
1	8						5	7
			8	2			4	
				3	7		1	
	3		2			6	7	
7	1		9					

	9	4			6		7	
		7	4					
		3			9	6		
7	2				3	4		1
	3						2	
4		5	1				3	7
		2	6			7		
					4	9		
	7		9			1	8	

4				8		3		1
	9	7					8	4
	8		5	7				
				2	8			9
	4	8				7	2	
9			1	3				
				4	2		1	
8	1					9	4	
5		4		6				7

	8			9			5	
	5	2			7	6	1	
1			3					
	9			6	1		4	5
		5				7		
8	7		5	4			6	
					3			7
	2	4	9			5	3	
	3			7			9	

1
1
1

	9	4			1	8		
6								4
	3			4		2		
1	4				2	3		5
	8		4		7		2	
2		3	5				8	7
		8		2			3	
3								8
		9	6			7	4	

1
1
2

				7	1			
6			5	3		8	9	
4			6					
2		7			5		6	9
	6						4	
9	4		3			7		5
					4			7
	1	4		8	3			6
			2	5				

5		7				2	8	
	3	6		5		7		
9	4		6					
	5		1	8				
6								1
				4	3		5	
					4		2	7
		8		9		1	3	
	2	3				9		5

7		6			8	5		3
		1						4
8	3	5			2			
			7			2		9
	8		1		4		6	
1		2			9			
			3			6	8	2
3						9		
6		8	2			3		7

	8			1	5	2	9	
7						1	8	
			2			6		
		1	8				2	
		9	7	4	2	5		
	2					9	3	
		8			1			
	1	3						2
	4	7	5	8			3	

		4	5	3		9	2	
				9			4	
		6				5		
	1					7	6	2
3			1		7			4
2	7	8					3	
		1				4		
	4			6				
		2	7		4	5	6	

117

	3	5			2		9	6
		2			3		4	
			6	7			3	
	2		7	4				1
6								3
9				6	8		2	
	1			9	6			
	9		4			2		
5	4		2			3	1	

118

		7		3			9	
9			2				1	7
			9			4		
	8	4		1				2
	6		7		9		8	
5				6		7	4	
		2			6			
3	9				5			4
	5			2		3		

				1				3
	6	3	2	9		4	1	
	9	1			5			
		7				8		
6	8		4		2		9	1
		4				5		
			6			7	4	
	1	6		3	7	2	8	
8				2				

		2	8	9	4		7	
7	5		1					
				3		2		
9		5				1		
2		1				3		8
		8				9		4
		6		8				
					9		3	1
	3		7	6	1	4		

				2	1	9		
2					8		6	
3				9			1	2
				8	6	2		3
8								9
6		2	9	3				
4	2			6				5
	5		7					6
		9	1	5				

	2				7		4	6
	4	7	3					
		1			2	3		
	8	2			4			
5	7			2			6	9
			1			4	8	
		3	5			7		
					9	6	5	
4	5		7				2	

	7	4	1		2			
	5			6		1		3
3								
		1	3				5	9
	3	5				6	4	
4	9				5	8		
								4
1		8		2			7	
			8		4	2	1	

9		8		3	4			
		3				5		2
	5			7	2		9	
1				4			6	7
	3						8	
6	8			9				5
	4		3	6			7	
3		9				6		
			4	1		8		3

		7						
1		6	5	3				
3				8		4	7	1
	8	9	6					3
	1			9			5	
2					3	6	8	
9	7	1		5				2
				6	8	9		7
						3		

	9	4	3	1				
	5				6			
3				7		9		
5		1	8			3		
	8	3		5		1	4	
		9			3	7		8
		5		9				3
			2				9	
				6	1	4	7	

127

3						6		8
		9			6		1	
6		5		4			2	
			4		9		3	5
		3	2		7	8		
5	2		3		8			
	9			2		3		4
	3		6			5		
7		2						1

128

|
9				7			4
		6			5	8		
		7		6		5		3
	8	4		9				
9			1		8			6
				7		4	8	
5		9		8		3		
		3	2			9		
6			7				1	

129

3				2				
		9						4
2	7		8			3	1	9
	2	3			9	7		
			3	6	1			
		1	2			9	4	
1	8	5			2		3	6
9						2		
				4				5

130

		7			1			
8	5		9			1		
6			5		3	9		2
			3				8	
1	6						2	3
	4				8			
9		1	2		5			6
		6			4		3	9
			8			7		

				9		3	5	2
1	3		8				9	7
			6					
5		6	1				7	
		2	6		3	9		
	9				8	2		6
			1					
2	4				5		6	1
6	5	1		3				

	9	1			6			3
3			2			6		
	7	2		9	3			
					2		9	
	2		5		9		4	
	1		4					
			3	2		5	6	
		7			8			4
4			9			2	1	

	5							8
				8	2		3	1
7					3	6	4	
5			4	3			2	
	4						8	
	9			6	1			7
	7	8	3					5
6	2		8	1				
4							1	

5	7						8	6
	1		6		3			
	8	6		9				
4	2	3						
8			3		9			2
						4	5	3
				5		7	2	
			1		6		3	
9	5						4	1

6	9				8			
		4	7					
1		7				8	2	9
5	3			7				4
4			8		1			3
8				4			9	1
3	6	2				9		7
					6	3		
			2				4	8

	4				1			
	7		4	2				
6		9					7	1
	6	2			4	3	5	
			5		2			
	1	5	9			7	4	
3	5					9		8
				9	5		3	
			8				6	

Puzzle 137

5	7			3		9	2	
	8				7			
		6	5				7	
6		3	8			4	5	
		7				1		
	1	4			9	7		3
	4				5	2		
			7				3	
	6	2		8			9	4

Puzzle 138

2				6	1	4		7
	7		4					5
			5	9	6			
		8			3			
3			6		5			9
			9			3		
		2	3	7				
8					6		3	
4		7	1	9				2

Puzzle 139

8	3	6			5			4
			3				7	6
7			6	8			1	
		5		4			9	
	7			9		3		
	4			3	8			2
1	8				2			
3			4			6	8	9

Puzzle 140

	5	9		4				
4						6		8
1			3		2			
	4	2		3				1
		5	1		8	4		
9				6		5	3	
			8		9			5
7		4						6
				2		1	7	

141

	3	7						
1					7		4	3
		8			5	7		1
8		5		2				
	1	9		7		4	6	
				3		5		8
2		3	9			1		
5	9		4					6
						2	9	

142

		9		1	5			
5								
		1			7	5	2	9
	3			7	6	1		2
2								6
6		5	3	8			9	
1	4	3	7			9		
								7
			4	5		3		

Puzzle 143

3		1	2			7		
		2		3		6		5
	7				6			
8				6			7	9
		6				8		
7	5			1				3
			6				3	
5		7		2		9		
		8			9	2		1

Puzzle 144

3	6		4					7
	8							2
	9	7		3				4
			7		4		1	
		1	6		5	8		
	5		1		3			
7				6		5	9	
6							3	
2					1		4	6

	3		7		5			
5			9	8				7
8	7	4						
		3			2	9		
	2	5				3	8	
		8	4			2		
						1	5	2
1				7	4			3
			5		9		6	

			1		3		9	7
		7					3	
1			5				8	
			2	9				8
6		9	4		8	7		1
8				3	7			
	8				2			6
	9					2		
7	1		3		5			

147

2		8	5	6		1		
			7	9				
		4				9		6
5			9			8	1	4
1								2
4	7	9			2			3
6		7				2		
				2	9			
		2		7	6	3		1

148

			7		2	3		6
					1			8
8		1		6	3	7		5
	4	6				2		
		5				1	6	
4		2	8	7		5		3
3			2					
9		8	3		5			

78

	7	9	6	5		2		
5						3		
	8		2	7				
				3		6	9	5
			1		7			
8	3	6		4				
			2	1			8	
		8						2
		5		8	6	7	3	

					9	1	6	
1		6	3	4				9
			1			5		8
			2		1	8	9	
	2	9	6		7			
7		4			6			
9				3	4	2		5
	3	5	9					

7	1	2		9		4		
9							6	7
		3		7			1	
1			4	2		7		
	2						5	
		5		6	7			4
	7			3		5		
2	5							3
		8		1		9	7	6

2					1	3	7	
	6					8		2
		4		7			5	
				2		5		1
	2	8	3		6	7	9	
7		9		4				
	8			6		9		
9		1					6	
	7	2	1					8

				3	5			
6		1	7		9			
	5	3		1				
1		4	3	9		8		
9								3
		6		4	8	9		2
				2		1	8	
			8		1	3		5
			9	6				

6		4	2					
	5	3	8				4	
				4		6	3	7
4				2	7			
		9				1		
			9	5				4
3	9	8		6				
	4				9	5	6	
					4	9		2

1				2		6		
6			8		9			
		4	6					1
	7				4	1		9
	1		7		2		6	
4		9	5				2	
9					5	7		
			1		6			8
		3		7				2

					6	9		1
2		6	4				5	7
				7	8	2		
		2		5			8	
			7		4			
	7			9		2		
	2	9	3					
7	8				5	4		2
5		4	8					

8				9	1			
4				8	3	2	1	
	3		2	4		8		
		9				5		
	2						7	
		4				3		
		8		7	5		6	
	7	3	4	6				9
			9	1				8

4			5			8		
	8	5	7	6	2			
		6		3	4			
9	7	3					4	
	1					3	8	9
			4	2		1		
			9	8	5	6	7	
		9			7			8

	5			4		8	3	2
				8	2	7		
9		8	7					
1	4	6			7			
			4			6	2	1
					8	4		6
		4	9	7				
3	6	1		2			7	

		3	5					7
						2	9	
7			2			6		
5	2	7	9		6	3		8
9		8	4		3	5	1	2
		2			4			3
	3	1						
8				7	4			

161

				8		3		2
	8		2				9	
2	4					6		
4		8			7		3	
	1	5				8	4	
	3		4			1		7
		3					2	1
	7				2		8	
5		6		1				

162

	5							2
2		8			7			9
7	6							
6		5	3		4	1		
	3			1	2		9	
		4	7		8	5		3
							4	6
4			8			9		7
3							1	

	9					6		7
					8		5	
				1	4	2		9
1		2		6	5		7	
	4						2	
	7		9	3		1		6
8		6	3	7				
	1		8					
9		7					1	

	3			8	6			
			3		1	5	6	9
		6						
3			6			9		5
	8	2				6	7	
6		5			9			1
						2		
5	4	8	7		3			
			4	6			5	

	4		1					5
2			3					
		1	2	5		6	7	3
	7	8	4					9
5					8	7	1	
6	2	5		1	3	4		
					5			8
4					9		3	

1	4			9	3	7	2	
	6		8					
		7	1					4
	8					9		
	2	5		8		1	4	
		3					5	
8					7	2		
					8		1	
	1	6	4	5			7	9

			6			4	8	9
					9	1		
	3	1			8			
3	5					7	1	
	9		2	3	7		5	
	2	7					9	6
			7			6	4	
		3	8					
5	4	2			1			

		4		5	8	9		6
3		9			4	5	7	
	1							
	4	3						1
2			1		3			9
8						7	4	
							2	
	8	2	4			3		5
4		5	9	2		1		

169

9			8	2			7	
					6			8
5	2				7			
1			4	8			6	
4		2				9		3
	7			3	5			2
			5				3	6
7			6					
	8			7	9			4

170

	7		9	1				
	8			3	5			1
	6	9				2		5
		5			1		6	8
6	4		7			3		
7		6				1	2	
4			1	2			9	
				6	3		5	

								9
3		5			4		2	
9		7		5		1	3	
2					8	9	7	
		6				2		
	9	8	6					1
	1	9		7		6		5
	2		1			3		7
5								

3			5				7	
			6	7	2	9		
	9		4				6	
		1	6	5				
	3	7		9		6	2	
				3	1	5		
	8				6		1	
	6	9	3	7				
	7				5			6

9	2		3					1
		8	1		2	6		
			8				2	
		2				4		
4	7		9	2	3		1	6
		3				9		
	4				1			
		1	7		9	5		
7					6		4	8

	5					8		
	1			6		9		4
4	2	7	8	1				
		3						5
2			4		3			6
9						3		
				4	1	7	6	8
7		4		8			3	
		6					2	

	5	3						
				3	2	4	1	5
		1		9	4			
	9		2			8	5	
7				8				3
	4	2			9		6	
			9	1		3		
9	3	8	6	4				
						5	9	

5		6	7			3		
		4	2				5	
	2			1				8
9			8					2
4		3				5		7
8					5			1
6				8			9	
	3				2	8		
		8			7	4		3

177

	5				6		2	
9	2					7		4
			9				1	
2			6					1
8	3	1		9		2	4	6
7					2			3
	8				7			
5		7					3	9
	6		1				8	

178

				1				6
		2	8			1		5
8				6	3		2	
3			4	9		6		
		9				3		
		7		3	8			9
	2		6	8				3
9		4			1	2		
1				4				

					1	2		
		1		9			5	
	3	9	4	8				6
				7		6		9
	9	8		6		7	4	
4		6		1				
6				2	7	4	8	
	8			3		9		
		2	5					

4			1	6			2	
	2				4	1		
9	5				7	3		
						5		
8		7	4		9	2		1
		9						
		5	7				1	2
		8	9				6	
	9			4	1			3

9	7		5	6			2	3
4	6		2	8				
		5						
				5	6			
	3	7				4	9	
			4	7				
						9		
			3	2			7	4
3	4			1	9		5	2

5							6	
	2				8		9	
			7	9		1		2
			1	8		6	3	5
		5				8		
2	8	3		6	7			
9		4		7	5			
	7		3				1	
	5							4

7	5				8		9	
		8		5				
9			3			5		
	6	5	2	7				
		9	6		1	2		
				9	4	3	8	
		4			6			1
				4		8		
	8		9				5	7

			7				1	9
						6	4	
1				6	9	5		7
3				5	7			
6		7	4		2	9		1
			6	9				2
8		5	3	2				6
	4	9						
7	3				1			

185

7	3							
1			4	7			8	
4			9		3		1	7
			3	5			2	
			8		9			
	8			1	7			
5	4		7		2			8
	7			3	4			6
							7	9

186

				5			2	9
6	4		3		9	8		
			7					
1	5						8	4
		7	1		4	2		
9	2						7	1
				3				
		8	6		7		1	3
7	1			8				

187

	9		3	2	7			
			1			7		
7					5	4	1	
3		9	5					
2		8		9		5		1
					2	8		3
	7	3	8					4
		4			1			
			2	3	4		5	

188

		8		9	1			
		1						5
	6		7		2		9	1
4		6		1				
8			2		6			3
				3		9		4
6	2		4		3		5	
5						3		
			8	6		2		

	9	6				4		
	7	5		8				
3			9					5
6	1				8			
8		2	4		7	3		6
			6				7	1
7					9			8
				2		5	3	
		8				9	6	

		3	4				2	8
			2				6	
	6				3			
3		6		5	4		8	
9	1						5	4
	5		7	1		6		9
			1				4	
	4				2			
6	2				7	9		

5					1	9		
		6		4	5	8	7	
	3		9					1
			8			6		
8			5		7			3
		1		3				
6					3		2	
	1	3	2	7		5		
		9	1					7

	7		8					
6		1	2			3	7	
							5	6
	3	7	6	9		8		
4				8				5
		9		2	7	6	1	
7	9							
	8	4			1	9		7
					2		8	

193

6					9			
7	1		6			3		
	3			2				1
3					5	9	8	
		6	1		3	4		
	9	7	8					6
1				7			5	
		8			6		1	4
			4					8

194

6	7			2	1			
			9				2	6
	9							
9		4		1		6		
	1	6	5		3	4	8	
		2		6		1		3
							3	
8	4				6			
			1	5			6	7

195

1			7	6				8
			8	4	5		2	
5				2				
					4	3	7	
	4	3				2	9	
	9	5	3					
				8				7
	3		5	1	7			
8				3	6			1

196

Column								
		1	5			7		
8			2	7				
6	2		1	3	9			
	9							7
	1	6				2	8	
7							9	
			4	2	7		5	9
				8	3			1
		4			5	3		

197

5		2		4				
	8		6		7		4	
1		7			9			
2	5	1		7			9	6
6	9			2		8	7	5
			4			7		3
	1		7		2		5	
				8		6		2

198

2				5		8		
	5	9		4			1	6
7					3		9	
			9	2	6		8	
9								4
	2		7	3	4			
	9		6					8
8	4			9		5	7	
		7		8				9

199

7	1		4					
		4		6				
			7	2		9		8
		7				3		9
2	9	3				7	8	5
5		1				4		
6		2		5	7			
				3		2		
					2		6	3

200

8						4		5
3		2		4		8		
	7			1				
5		6	7			1		8
	4						9	
1		8			4	2		7
				2			6	
		4		5		7		2
2		1						4

201

6		2		1				7
	7	4						
			3	7				1
		6	8		2		1	5
5								3
3	1		5		7	2		
8				2	5			
						5	4	
7				4		8		2

202

4	7			3				9
		3	4		5			7
				7				
		9	1	5			6	3
8								5
3	5			4	6	1		
				8				
1			9		4	5		
5				6			2	8

		5						7
	1				8		9	
	7	9	6	4		3	1	
			7		4		2	
			9		3			
	9		5		6			
	4	8		9	1	5	6	
	6		4				3	
9						1		

	3						2	8
4					6	3	9	
	2	7	3	1			5	
		9		6				
2		4				8		9
				2		5		
	7			9	3	4	8	
	9	5	6					7
8	4						6	

Puzzle 205:

				1	2	7		5
2							8	4
			9	8	1	6		
			2				4	8
3			8		7			1
1	8		4					
	2	8	1	5				
9	3							6
4		1	9	7				

Puzzle 206:

3			8	6				7
		9	3	2		8		
		5					6	
	1						9	
9	7	6				5	3	1
	3						8	
	5					3		
		2		3	4	6		
6				1	8			5

				4		6	8	
8		2		3			1	9
			9					7
7	6				9			5
			7		5			
4			8				9	6
2					4			
9	8			7		1		2
	5	1		9				

3		7	6	9				
4	9		8	1				
	5		2					
6		9					8	
8	1						7	2
	2					1		6
					2		6	
				7	4		2	1
				6	8	7		3

			7			8	2	
	5	7	6					9
1				8	4		7	
				6			1	
		1	4	3	5	9		
	7			1				
	9		1	5				4
5					6	7	8	
	4	8			2			

	1					8		
6	4	2		7		9	3	
	7			6	3			4
		4			8		5	1
1	5		6			4		
7			9	2			4	
	2	5		1		3	7	8
		1					9	

3				1	5			7
			4	9	6	1		3
9		6			7			
		3			2			
7								9
			7			8		
			2			3		1
8		7	6	4	1			
1			9	5				4

9	5			1	6			7
		7		4	2		8	
		1						
			6	7		3	5	4
3	6	2	5	8				
						5		
	9		6	3		7		
5			1	7			4	8

		6	3		1			
5	3		9					2
	1		6	7			8	
		2	4					1
	9	8				4	5	
1					6	2		
	5			9	2		1	
4					3		2	8
			1		4	5		

	1	5	2					
	9	7	6	8				
6				9	1		7	
8	2							5
	5			2			6	
1							9	8
	6		9	3				7
				5	6	9	2	
					7	4	5	

215

	1		4		2		9	
9	8			7	5			
		4	1					7
4	6			5		9		
	9						5	
		5		2			4	3
3					4	1		
			7	8			2	9
	5		2		9		3	

216

		8	6		1		9	3
		4	8			2		
	2							7
		1			2		3	
	7		5		6		4	
	8		7			5		
2							5	
		5			3	9		
9	6		2		8	3		

		3				4		5
		6	3				1	
9	1	5			6	8		7
6					2			
	8			9			4	
			7					9
3		8	2			1	9	4
	6				5	7		
7		1				5		

		9	4	5		6		1
				9		7		
	3	8						5
			6				9	
2	7		3		9		6	8
	9				1			
9						3	4	
		7		2				
1		2		3	4	5		

219

	3		5	4				2
4	8				9			
9						6		3
2		3					6	5
	6		1		3		9	
5	9					7		1
8		5						9
			8				7	6
3				9	1		5	

220

							9	
		3		7	4	5	1	
					3	7	8	6
				2	8		6	
3		6				8		7
	1		3	5				
1	6	2	9					
	8	7	6	1		9		
	3							

221

1		6		5	3			2
	8				2		6	
7		2		8				
	2				6		4	
3								5
	1		8				2	
				7		9		6
	9		5				7	
6			3	2		1		8

222

	2		6					4
3	7				9		1	
6					7	5		
4		6	3					1
			5		6			
2					8	9		6
		9	7					2
	8		9				3	5
5					4		9	

223

9				8		7	1	
2	1	3	6		5			9
		8	7				5	
		7	1	5	2	4		
	4				8	1		
6			2		9	3	7	5
	5	2		3				1

224

3	5			6			2	
		6		9			3	
		2	4					1
	7						1	8
5	2		1		3		4	9
1	3						7	
2					9	1		
	6			5		7		
	8			1			9	3

225

				9	8	7		
		6			2			4
			7			3	2	
4	9				5			3
7		3				1		5
6			1				8	9
	2	4			7			
3			2			5		
		7	8	3				

226

9			1			2	6	
				9	6			
			5	3				9
	2	4		1		5	3	
6	9						4	1
	3	8		5		9	2	
2				6	5			
			3	4				
	1	6			9			5

	2		1				7	
			2	7			9	4
		8		3	4			1
		3	4			6	5	
	8	7			9	1		
8			9	6		4		
7	6			4	2			
	9				1		2	

			8	1		7	4	
1					6	8		5
	8			3				
9	6				4			2
	3			8			6	
2			9				5	7
				5			9	
8		5	1					3
	2	6		9	7			

					9		6	
9		4	5		2	3	1	
		2			8		9	
	3		4			6		2
7		6			1		5	
	9		1			4		
	1	3	2		4	8		9
	2		6					

	5							9
	9				8	6		
		7	5	9	6			
9		8					3	
6	7		9		5		8	2
	1					4		7
			2	5	4	3		
		4	6				7	
2							6	

2			1	5		9		
7					8			1
	1			3	7	2		
				9			5	
	2		8		5		9	
	6			7				
		3	7	4			2	
4			6					5
		9		2	3			6

2 3 1

6					3	8		
5		2					9	
8	4				5	1		6
		5		2		4		3
4		1		8		5		
7		9	1				4	8
	3					7		5
		8	4					9

2 3 2

			6	4			3	8
6						1		5
		8						
3		1			2		9	
8	7	2				6	5	1
	9		7			3		2
						8		
9		3						7
1	2			3	6			

7	1					6		4
		9			1			3
	5		7		4	1		
				3		2		1
		2				8		
6		1		7				
		3	6		9		8	
8			5			3		
5		7					1	9

2 3 5

	4			5		8	2	
7				2		5		
8	5		9					
	6				4		5	8
1			5		7			6
3	8		6				7	
					2		9	1
		1		7				3
	7	6		9			8	

2 3 6

			1	6				
	2					1	3	
		3	2	8		7		6
1					8	6	2	
4								9
	5	8	6					7
8		1		3	5	9		
	7	9					4	
				4	1			

6			7			8	4	
4		9	5					
3		5		6				
9		4	3				8	
	5						2	
	1				9	3		6
				7		4		2
					1	5		7
	9	7			5			8

9				4		1		
	8				5	3	9	
	7	3						
			2	5	1	9	4	
5				9				6
	4	9	7	6	3			
						5	2	
	1	8	5				3	
		5		7				4

		8			5			7
7	2	1	9					6
	4	5					3	
			3		7		6	
1								5
	5		2		1			
	6					9	4	
2					6	3	7	8
3			1			6		

1	7			3		5		4
	4				6			
		3	4	7				
	6				2		9	3
	9	5				4	1	
7	3		1				5	
				8	3	2		
			5				7	
2		7		9			3	8

2 4 1

		6				7		
			9	6				5
		8		2	4			9
			6		9	5		3
7								8
5		9	8		3			
1			4	3		2		
8				1	7			
		3				1		

2 4 2

3	8				4	2		7
				8	3			
	1				7			3
		2					7	
	6		7	3	2		5	
	5					6		
5			6				1	
			4	2				
4		7	3				6	9

6							1	
4	7	2				6	9	
		1	8					5
			3				7	
		9	6	5	2	8		
	1				9			
1					5	4		
	8	5				1	2	6
	9							3

2					1	5		4
		1		6			2	
9						1	3	
					3	8		5
			6		7			
7		4	1					
	7	5						9
	8			3		2		
3		9	5					7

								1
	8		3				4	9
			9		5	8		
		6			9		3	8
2			4	6	8			5
4	9		3			1		
	2	1		7				
7	4			2			6	
6								

		4	6					7
			5					
1		5					6	2
	5	8	1		6		3	
	7						8	
	4		2		3	7	1	
9	6					8		4
				9				
4				5	9			

	2	5		6			3	
		3	9				6	
	6			4				2
			7					6
5	1						7	4
2					1			
8				3			1	
	3				9	7		
	4			5		6	8	

					2	9		3
3		6		5				
		9			1		7	6
				8		4	1	
				6				
	5	2		9				
4	2		9			7		
				7		8		2
5		3	4					

249

		3	6		1			
	2		8		3			9
		5			9			2
						1	5	4
6								3
4	9	1						
5			1			6		
1			2		6		8	
			5		8	2		

250

			3	9		6	1	
			7					3
				8	1	7	2	
2	7							1
4								5
3							8	2
	3	8	1	2				
1					8			
	5	2		6	4			

							7	6
2							4	8
6				4	8	3		9
			6	7		1		
	4			8			9	
		2		5	1			
7		1	4	9				3
5	6							1
9	2							

9	1					3		
					7	1		
			4			9		8
		3		7	4		1	
8				1				3
	5		2	6		8		
2		4			5			
		9	1					
		8					3	2

2 5 3

				7			8	4
2				4	3			9
	7	6						2
5	3				9			
		7				1		
			2				7	5
7						8	9	
8			1	5				6
6	1			8				

2 5 4

3			2					
2		9	6		8		5	
			1					
9	6	2			5	7		
		7				1		
		4	9			6	3	2
					9			
	7		5		6	9		4
					1			3

				9	2	5		7
					3	6	2	4
			4	1				
	4	1		2		7		
		9		3		1	5	
				4	9			
2	9	4	8					
8		5	3	7				

8	2	9					6	
							4	
	3			9	1			5
			7	2		1	5	
			5	6	3			
	9	3		4	8			
4			2	3			1	
	8							
	5					7	3	4

2 5 7

					6	9		8
			7	2			6	3
							4	
1	2				8		3	
5	4						8	9
	8		3				1	6
	1							
8	3			5	4			
7		9	1					

2 5 8

				9		4		
4					6	2	3	9
1		9						
		1		5		6		
7				6				2
		8	2			9		
						7		3
8	4	2	3					5
		7		1				

259

		1			3		4	
	6			2		1		
	4	3	7					
6		7			5			
		2		4		9		
			6			2		8
					1	4	7	
		6		8			9	
	9		5			6		

260

9		4	6					7
		8					5	
			8		1		6	
				8			7	1
			7	4	3			
7	2			5				
	5		2		4			
	7					5		
1					8	7		2

		5	3	2		4		
					9		2	
1		9				5	3	
2							7	
5		3		9		8		2
	6							9
	7	4				2		1
	3		7					
		2		4	8	7		

	9		7			4		5
7	6			3	1			
5		2	9					
6			1					7
4					9			1
					2	6		8
			4	1			2	9
9		5			8		1	

263

7		1				3		
	4	6		7				
						4		9
		8		9	6	1		
9				1				8
		5	8	4		9		
8		2						
				8		6	3	
		7				5		1

264

					5	4		1
			7				6	
6		3	9	8				
7			5					
2	3			1			4	8
					4			5
				5	9	2		7
	5				2			
9		7	1					

	6						5	
			6			7		9
2	7		1				4	
4	9	3	8					
7				6				2
					3	9	7	8
	4				1		8	3
1		2			4			
	8						9	

	9		2					1
				8				
		2	1		7		3	
		3		4	1	6	7	
	1			3			4	
	4	7	6	2		8		
	5		8		3	9		
				6				
6					5		8	

	6		4	9			7	
	7	3				9		2
								5
6		2			3			
	9	1		8		6	2	
			2			5		3
7								
8		5				2	1	
	2			1	8		5	

2	6	8						
			2		4	7		
				9				2
7	3		6				8	5
	4			3			2	
8	5				1		4	3
1			7					
		3	4		6			
						5	3	9

	4		7	9	8			
		2	5	3			6	
	5	7						
2		5						
3			4	6	9			5
						8		1
						9	3	
	6			1	3	2		
			2	5	4		7	

		5	1				4	
		6	9				3	5
1	4							
7	5				4			
	6		2		4		5	
		8					9	2
							1	3
2	1				8	6		
	7				6	2		

6		7	9		3		2	
2		5			1			6
			6					
4							8	
	7	8				4	1	
	2							5
				4				
9			2			7		4
	4		7		9	3		1

		8				5		
		3	4					6
1				8	5			
				3		6		1
2	3			7			4	5
4		5		2				
			8	9				4
9					6	3		
		2				8		

						1	7	
		1	4	8				
	4		5	9		3		
	5		8		3	7		
1								6
		8	7		2		9	
		6		5	9		3	
			7	4	2			
	3	4						

		5		7				9
			1		4			
	2	8					1	
3		7		8		4	5	
				6				
	9	1		2		6		3
	5					2	9	
			6		7			
1				4		5		

Puzzle 275

5				9	8	6	7	
4								8
	6				2	3		
9	8		1					
3								7
				3			9	2
		5	2				8	
6								1
	9	7	4	8				3

Puzzle 276

			9		7		4	
					8	7	5	
	9		1			3	8	
	2	1	5			9		
				2				
		6			4	5	2	
	5	2			9		7	
	6	7	3					
	3		7		6			

142

7			1	9	6			
	1	6		3				
3	9							5
9	8		2					
	7						4	
					4		2	9
5							6	8
				5		4	3	
			4	8	3			2

	3	8			7			
5					1		8	4
		1		2		6		
1							4	
	9		7		6		2	
	7							9
		6		1		5		
3	1		5					2
			4			3	9	

3					6	8	5	
7							1	
	5	2		3				
			4	2		3		
	4		8		7		9	
		1		9	3			
				1		7	6	
	7							4
	3	8	9					1

	3	1	2			7	4	
		7	8			2		
	2		9		4		8	
								4
2				6				5
3								
	5		4		7		6	
		2			3	5		
	1	3			8	4	9	

		8		3	4		9	
			6			8		
9	2					6		3
	8	1	7					
			9	8	2			
					3	2	5	
3		6					4	9
		5			1			
	1		3	9		5		

1	8						2	
	7				1			
2			3			6	1	
			9	5	2	7		
	5						8	
		7	6	8	4			
	3	5			6			8
			5				6	
	9						7	2

1		8	3			9		
	4	7	5	8			6	
5		3						
			2				4	
7				1				9
	2				6			
						3		4
	3			9	1	8	2	
		2			5	7		1

1		8			4			6
	2	6		1				5
			7					8
9	5							
	3		8		2		1	
							3	7
2					9			
8				3		4	2	
3			2			7		1

Puzzle 285

4							3	2
					8			6
	3			6	9	5		4
8		2				1		
	5						7	
		4				6		5
1		5	6	8			4	
3			9					
2	8							9

Puzzle 286

			3	4		5	1	9
						6		
4			1		8			7
		2					8	5
		8				1		
7	5					3		
8			6		9			1
		9						
1	7	5		3	2			

			6		1		5	
		1						8
5		9	2	8			3	
8		3					7	
			4		2			
	4					6		2
	5			6	4	9		7
7						1		
	8		5		9			

	1			2	9		8	
		2						6
		9	6	1				3
		5			6			
		7	9		1	5		
			3			9		
9				4	2	6		
3						8		
	5		1	6			4	

	2					9		4
						5	1	
1		7	2					
	1	6	7	8			9	
5				3				8
	8			2	1	7	3	
					3	4		1
	6	1						
2		9					6	

8				4	2		1	3
	7					2		
3					6		9	
	6							5
	3	9				4	8	
1							6	
	9		2					1
		7					5	
6	4		1	5				9

291

		5						
						2	9	
1		4		2		6		8
8	4	2		1	3	9		
				5				
		6	4	9		7	1	2
2		8		4		1		7
	3	1						
						3		

292

				6		5	2	
			4			1		
1	9	3					8	
	3			9	2	6		1
8		9	6	3			5	
	6					7	4	3
		7			3			
	8	4		2				

Puzzle 293:

		1	4					
6				8				
	8	9	3				6	5
	9					8		
3		5	8		4	9		6
		4					7	
1	4				7	3	2	
				2				7
					3	1		

Puzzle 294:

				4			9	5
						8		6
		8	5					
5	1		9		7			8
6		2		8		5		9
8			6		2		3	1
					6	2		
3		7						
9	5			7				

Puzzle 295:

	5						8	
	1		4			3		
	7	6		2	8		1	
6			7	9				
4				3				7
				5	2			9
	6		5	8		7	4	
		1			9		2	
	8						9	

Puzzle 296:

						6		2
		4					1	
2			5	3	1			
8		7	1		3		9	
	5			8			4	
	6		7		9	1		8
			4	7	2			1
	2					7		
7		1						

9		7		2		1	3	
	1		6			2		
			9					8
5		3					8	
	9						4	
	8					3		5
2					7			
		4			8		7	
	3	8		6		5		2

3		2			1			5
			7	2	5		8	
		6					2	
			5	9				
4	6						5	7
				7	6			
	3					6		
	4		2	8	9			
9			1			7		8

					9	7	4	1
	3		7		2			8
	4		6			5		
						2	9	
9								4
	2	6						
		1		4		8		
4			3	7		5		
6	7	3	9					

7	4				9		3	
6			5				7	
1	3			2				6
	6					9		
2				4				8
		4				5		
4				5			1	3
	5				8			4
	7		6				9	5

1

2	9	3	8	4	1	6	5	7
7	5	8	9	6	3	4	1	2
6	1	4	5	2	7	3	9	8
1	3	5	6	7	9	2	8	4
9	4	2	3	8	5	1	7	6
8	6	7	2	1	4	9	3	5
5	2	6	1	3	8	7	4	9
3	7	9	4	5	6	8	2	1
4	8	1	7	9	2	5	6	3

2

4	9	2	6	1	5	8	7	3
8	7	6	2	3	9	4	1	5
3	1	5	4	8	7	6	2	9
7	2	9	8	6	1	5	3	4
1	5	8	9	4	3	2	6	7
6	4	3	5	7	2	1	9	8
9	8	7	1	5	6	3	4	2
5	3	1	7	2	4	9	8	6
2	6	4	3	9	8	7	5	1

3

8	7	3	1	6	9	5	2	4
6	9	2	8	5	4	1	7	3
5	1	4	3	7	2	9	6	8
9	6	5	7	4	1	8	3	2
2	4	8	5	9	3	6	1	7
1	3	7	2	8	6	4	9	5
4	5	9	6	2	7	3	8	1
7	8	1	9	3	5	2	4	6
3	2	6	4	1	8	7	5	9

4

9	6	3	5	4	1	8	2	7
5	8	7	6	2	3	4	1	9
4	1	2	8	7	9	6	3	5
3	9	1	7	8	4	5	6	2
2	4	8	1	6	5	7	9	3
7	5	6	3	9	2	1	4	8
8	3	9	4	5	6	2	7	1
6	2	5	9	1	7	3	8	4
1	7	4	2	3	8	9	5	6

5

5	9	3	8	7	1	4	2	6
7	2	1	5	4	6	3	8	9
6	4	8	9	2	3	7	1	5
3	5	2	7	6	9	8	4	1
8	1	7	4	3	5	6	9	2
9	6	4	1	8	2	5	7	3
2	7	6	3	1	8	9	5	4
4	3	9	2	5	7	1	6	8
1	8	5	6	9	4	2	3	7

6

7	4	6	1	5	2	9	8	3
2	3	1	6	9	8	5	7	4
9	8	5	3	7	4	1	6	2
6	2	3	7	8	5	4	1	9
8	9	4	2	1	6	7	3	5
5	1	7	9	4	3	8	2	6
1	7	2	4	3	9	6	5	8
3	5	9	8	6	1	2	4	7
4	6	8	5	2	7	3	9	1

7

3	9	6	4	2	8	7	1	5
7	4	2	1	5	6	9	8	3
5	8	1	3	9	7	4	6	2
4	1	7	9	3	5	8	2	6
2	6	5	8	7	1	3	4	9
9	3	8	2	6	4	1	5	7
8	5	9	6	4	3	2	7	1
1	7	3	5	8	2	6	9	4
6	2	4	7	1	9	5	3	8

8

3	2	4	6	7	1	5	8	9
8	5	1	3	9	4	6	7	2
9	7	6	8	5	2	1	3	4
2	6	3	9	1	7	4	5	8
1	8	9	4	3	5	7	2	6
7	4	5	2	6	8	9	1	3
4	9	7	1	8	3	2	6	5
6	1	8	5	2	9	3	4	7
5	3	2	7	4	6	8	9	1

9

5	6	2	9	7	8	1	3	4
8	4	3	1	6	2	7	5	9
1	9	7	4	5	3	2	6	8
9	3	1	7	8	6	5	4	2
6	5	8	2	9	4	3	7	1
7	2	4	3	1	5	8	9	6
4	8	9	5	3	1	6	2	7
2	1	5	6	4	7	9	8	3
3	7	6	8	2	9	4	1	5

10

7	5	1	3	4	9	2	6	8
8	2	3	7	1	6	9	4	5
4	6	9	5	2	8	1	3	7
6	1	7	2	8	3	4	5	9
9	8	4	1	7	5	3	2	6
5	3	2	6	9	4	7	8	1
2	9	8	4	6	7	5	1	3
3	4	6	9	5	1	8	7	2
1	7	5	8	3	2	6	9	4

11

2	8	5	6	4	9	1	3	7
1	3	9	8	2	7	4	6	5
4	6	7	3	5	1	9	8	2
5	7	1	2	8	3	6	9	4
6	2	8	4	9	5	7	1	3
3	9	4	1	7	6	5	2	8
9	1	2	5	3	4	8	7	6
8	4	6	7	1	2	3	5	9
7	5	3	9	6	8	2	4	1

12

8	1	4	6	5	3	7	9	2
5	7	6	8	9	2	3	1	4
9	3	2	1	7	4	6	8	5
2	6	7	3	4	9	8	5	1
1	9	8	5	2	6	4	7	3
4	5	3	7	8	1	9	2	6
6	2	1	9	3	7	5	4	8
7	4	5	2	6	8	1	3	9
3	8	9	4	1	5	2	6	7

13

5	1	7	3	4	8	6	2	9
6	8	3	2	9	1	7	4	5
4	9	2	7	5	6	1	8	3
8	3	6	4	7	2	5	9	1
9	7	4	6	1	5	2	3	8
2	5	1	9	8	3	4	6	7
1	6	8	5	3	4	9	7	2
7	2	5	8	6	9	3	1	4
3	4	9	1	2	7	8	5	6

14

5	8	9	1	4	3	7	2	6
4	2	1	8	7	6	3	5	9
3	6	7	5	2	9	4	8	1
2	5	6	7	3	1	9	4	8
9	1	8	6	5	4	2	7	3
7	4	3	2	9	8	1	6	5
8	9	2	3	6	7	5	1	4
1	7	4	9	8	5	6	3	2
6	3	5	4	1	2	8	9	7

15

8	2	7	3	5	4	9	1	6
6	5	4	9	7	1	2	3	8
3	1	9	6	2	8	7	5	4
4	9	5	1	8	6	3	2	7
7	6	3	2	4	5	8	9	1
2	8	1	7	9	3	6	4	5
1	4	2	8	3	7	5	6	9
9	7	6	5	1	2	4	8	3
5	3	8	4	6	9	1	7	2

16

2	5	3	4	7	9	6	1	8
7	8	1	6	5	3	4	2	9
6	4	9	2	1	8	5	7	3
8	6	4	3	2	1	9	5	7
9	1	7	8	4	5	2	3	6
3	2	5	9	6	7	1	8	4
4	7	8	1	9	2	3	6	5
1	3	6	5	8	4	7	9	2
5	9	2	7	3	6	8	4	1

17

3	5	2	7	1	9	4	8	6
9	6	8	4	3	5	2	7	1
7	4	1	6	2	8	5	9	3
8	2	7	1	5	6	9	3	4
5	1	6	9	4	3	8	2	7
4	9	3	2	8	7	6	1	5
6	7	4	3	9	2	1	5	8
2	3	5	8	6	1	7	4	9
1	8	9	5	7	4	3	6	2

18

9	7	8	1	5	6	4	3	2
1	5	3	4	8	2	7	9	6
6	4	2	9	3	7	1	5	8
2	6	9	5	1	8	3	7	4
4	8	5	7	2	3	6	1	9
3	1	7	6	4	9	2	8	5
5	9	6	3	7	4	8	2	1
8	3	4	2	9	1	5	6	7
7	2	1	8	6	5	9	4	3

19

3	7	2	8	6	1	9	4	5
5	4	6	7	9	3	1	8	2
1	9	8	2	4	5	3	7	6
7	3	1	5	8	2	4	6	9
2	5	4	6	7	9	8	3	1
8	6	9	1	3	4	5	2	7
4	1	7	3	5	6	2	9	8
6	2	3	9	1	8	7	5	4
9	8	5	4	2	7	6	1	3

20

3	4	1	9	8	5	6	2	7
2	5	9	7	6	3	1	4	8
8	7	6	1	2	4	3	9	5
5	2	4	3	1	6	7	8	9
6	8	7	5	9	2	4	1	3
1	9	3	4	7	8	5	6	2
4	3	2	8	5	1	9	7	6
9	6	5	2	4	7	8	3	1
7	1	8	6	3	9	2	5	4

21

2	4	9	8	1	7	3	5	6
5	1	7	6	3	4	9	8	2
6	3	8	2	5	9	1	4	7
4	2	6	5	7	3	8	1	9
7	9	5	1	2	8	4	6	3
3	8	1	9	4	6	2	7	5
1	6	2	3	8	5	7	9	4
8	5	4	7	9	2	6	3	1
9	7	3	4	6	1	5	2	8

22

9	8	7	1	5	3	6	4	2
6	4	2	8	9	7	1	3	5
3	1	5	4	2	6	9	7	8
2	9	6	7	8	4	3	5	1
4	3	1	2	6	5	7	8	9
5	7	8	3	1	9	4	2	6
1	5	3	6	7	2	8	9	4
8	2	4	9	3	1	5	6	7
7	6	9	5	4	8	2	1	3

23

7	8	4	9	2	1	5	6	3
9	6	5	7	3	8	4	2	1
2	1	3	5	6	4	7	8	9
6	7	1	2	8	3	9	4	5
4	5	9	6	1	7	2	3	8
3	2	8	4	9	5	1	7	6
8	9	7	1	4	6	3	5	2
5	3	2	8	7	9	6	1	4
1	4	6	3	5	2	8	9	7

24

5	6	9	4	2	1	3	8	7
8	7	3	5	6	9	2	4	1
4	1	2	8	3	7	6	9	5
1	5	6	9	4	8	7	2	3
9	3	4	1	7	2	8	5	6
7	2	8	3	5	6	9	1	4
3	8	7	2	1	4	5	6	9
2	4	5	6	9	3	1	7	8
6	9	1	7	8	5	4	3	2

25

7	9	6	2	4	1	8	3	5
8	5	4	9	7	3	6	2	1
2	1	3	5	8	6	7	4	9
4	8	2	7	5	9	1	6	3
1	6	9	3	2	4	5	7	8
3	7	5	1	6	8	4	9	2
6	2	1	4	9	5	3	8	7
5	4	7	8	3	2	9	1	6
9	3	8	6	1	7	2	5	4

26

2	4	1	5	8	6	9	3	7
7	6	3	4	1	9	8	2	5
8	5	9	3	2	7	4	6	1
4	9	5	2	6	8	1	7	3
6	8	7	9	3	1	2	5	4
3	1	2	7	5	4	6	9	8
1	7	8	6	9	5	3	4	2
5	3	6	1	4	2	7	8	9
9	2	4	8	7	3	5	1	6

27

9	2	6	8	1	3	4	7	5
8	4	5	9	7	6	1	3	2
3	7	1	5	4	2	6	9	8
2	5	4	7	3	8	9	6	1
7	6	8	1	9	5	2	4	3
1	9	3	6	2	4	5	8	7
6	1	7	3	5	9	8	2	4
5	8	2	4	6	7	3	1	9
4	3	9	2	8	1	7	5	6

28

2	9	5	7	4	1	6	3	8
6	1	8	9	3	2	7	5	4
7	4	3	5	6	8	2	1	9
9	7	4	6	8	3	5	2	1
3	8	1	2	5	7	9	4	6
5	2	6	4	1	9	3	8	7
1	5	7	8	2	6	4	9	3
4	3	9	1	7	5	8	6	2
8	6	2	3	9	4	1	7	5

29

8	4	7	2	3	1	9	5	6
1	5	2	6	4	9	7	3	8
9	6	3	5	7	8	1	2	4
6	2	1	4	9	5	3	8	7
3	9	4	7	8	2	6	1	5
7	8	5	1	6	3	4	9	2
2	3	6	8	1	4	5	7	9
5	7	9	3	2	6	8	4	1
4	1	8	9	5	7	2	6	3

30

8	4	7	5	6	2	9	3	1
2	6	9	3	1	8	4	7	5
3	5	1	4	7	9	2	8	6
7	1	3	9	5	6	8	4	2
6	9	2	8	4	7	5	1	3
4	8	5	2	3	1	6	9	7
1	7	4	6	9	5	3	2	8
9	2	6	7	8	3	1	5	4
5	3	8	1	2	4	7	6	9

31

2	4	5	1	6	7	9	3	8
7	6	9	5	8	3	1	4	2
1	8	3	9	4	2	6	5	7
9	2	7	8	1	5	3	6	4
4	3	6	2	7	9	5	8	1
5	1	8	6	3	4	7	2	9
3	9	4	7	5	8	2	1	6
6	5	2	4	9	1	8	7	3
8	7	1	3	2	6	4	9	5

32

5	2	6	1	4	9	7	8	3
3	1	4	6	8	7	9	2	5
8	9	7	2	3	5	6	1	4
4	8	2	7	1	6	3	5	9
1	7	9	3	5	4	8	6	2
6	5	3	8	9	2	1	4	7
9	3	1	5	2	8	4	7	6
2	6	8	4	7	3	5	9	1
7	4	5	9	6	1	2	3	8

33

8	1	5	3	7	9	6	2	4
9	7	4	2	5	6	1	3	8
2	3	6	4	8	1	5	7	9
5	8	7	6	3	4	2	9	1
1	6	9	5	2	8	3	4	7
3	4	2	9	1	7	8	5	6
7	9	3	8	6	2	4	1	5
4	2	8	1	9	5	7	6	3
6	5	1	7	4	3	9	8	2

34

1	5	8	9	3	4	2	6	7
4	7	2	8	6	5	1	9	3
9	3	6	1	7	2	5	8	4
8	4	7	6	1	3	9	2	5
5	6	9	2	8	7	4	3	1
3	2	1	4	5	9	6	7	8
7	1	5	3	9	6	8	4	2
2	9	3	5	4	8	7	1	6
6	8	4	7	2	1	3	5	9

35

2	3	6	7	1	4	9	8	5
5	8	1	3	2	9	7	4	6
9	7	4	8	6	5	1	2	3
3	2	5	9	7	1	4	6	8
6	9	7	4	5	8	3	1	2
4	1	8	2	3	6	5	7	9
8	4	3	1	9	2	6	5	7
1	5	9	6	8	7	2	3	4
7	6	2	5	4	3	8	9	1

36

9	7	2	3	1	8	4	6	5
8	5	1	4	6	9	7	2	3
6	3	4	2	5	7	1	8	9
4	9	7	1	2	6	3	5	8
5	1	8	9	7	3	6	4	2
2	6	3	5	8	4	9	7	1
7	4	5	8	9	1	2	3	6
1	8	6	7	3	2	5	9	4
3	2	9	6	4	5	8	1	7

37

2	8	1	7	9	5	3	6	4
9	4	3	8	2	6	5	1	7
5	6	7	3	1	4	2	9	8
7	1	6	2	3	8	9	4	5
3	2	5	6	4	9	8	7	1
8	9	4	1	5	7	6	2	3
4	5	2	9	7	3	1	8	6
1	7	8	5	6	2	4	3	9
6	3	9	4	8	1	7	5	2

38

1	4	3	7	9	6	8	2	5
9	8	7	4	2	5	6	3	1
6	2	5	1	8	3	7	9	4
3	9	6	2	4	7	1	5	8
8	5	1	6	3	9	2	4	7
4	7	2	5	1	8	9	6	3
5	6	4	8	7	2	3	1	9
2	3	8	9	5	1	4	7	6
7	1	9	3	6	4	5	8	2

39

2	1	9	5	6	3	7	4	8
8	7	4	1	9	2	5	6	3
3	5	6	7	8	4	2	1	9
4	3	7	8	2	6	9	5	1
6	8	5	9	7	1	4	3	2
1	9	2	4	3	5	6	8	7
9	6	1	3	4	7	8	2	5
7	4	3	2	5	8	1	9	6
5	2	8	6	1	9	3	7	4

40

3	9	7	8	6	1	2	5	4
6	5	4	9	7	2	3	8	1
1	2	8	3	4	5	9	7	6
7	8	1	5	2	6	4	3	9
9	6	2	4	3	8	5	1	7
5	4	3	7	1	9	8	6	2
8	1	9	6	5	4	7	2	3
2	3	5	1	9	7	6	4	8
4	7	6	2	8	3	1	9	5

4 1

3	2	4	7	8	9	6	5	1
1	9	6	4	5	2	8	3	7
8	5	7	6	3	1	2	4	9
7	4	1	8	2	3	9	6	5
2	3	5	9	4	6	7	1	8
9	6	8	5	1	7	3	2	4
4	1	3	2	9	8	5	7	6
5	7	9	3	6	4	1	8	2
6	8	2	1	7	5	4	9	3

4 2

1	7	3	6	2	5	8	9	4
4	5	6	8	9	3	2	1	7
9	2	8	4	7	1	3	5	6
6	9	7	2	4	8	1	3	5
8	3	2	1	5	6	4	7	9
5	1	4	9	3	7	6	2	8
3	8	1	7	6	9	5	4	2
7	4	5	3	8	2	9	6	1
2	6	9	5	1	4	7	8	3

4 3

5	7	9	8	1	2	6	3	4
6	8	3	7	9	4	5	1	2
1	2	4	6	3	5	9	8	7
7	9	8	1	5	3	2	4	6
3	4	5	2	6	7	1	9	8
2	1	6	9	4	8	3	7	5
9	6	2	4	7	1	8	5	3
4	3	1	5	8	6	7	2	9
8	5	7	3	2	9	4	6	1

4 4

8	1	3	7	2	4	5	9	6
2	5	9	1	6	8	7	4	3
7	4	6	3	5	9	8	2	1
5	9	8	4	3	2	1	6	7
4	6	2	5	7	1	9	3	8
3	7	1	9	8	6	2	5	4
9	3	4	2	1	7	6	8	5
1	8	5	6	9	3	4	7	2
6	2	7	8	4	5	3	1	9

4 5

1	6	5	9	2	3	7	8	4
8	4	9	7	1	6	2	3	5
2	7	3	5	4	8	9	6	1
3	2	6	4	9	1	8	5	7
5	9	1	8	6	7	4	2	3
4	8	7	2	3	5	6	1	9
7	3	4	6	5	2	1	9	8
9	5	2	1	8	4	3	7	6
6	1	8	3	7	9	5	4	2

4 6

8	7	2	3	6	5	9	4	1
5	1	4	8	9	2	7	6	3
3	9	6	7	4	1	5	2	8
4	6	1	2	7	8	3	9	5
2	3	5	6	1	9	8	7	4
7	8	9	4	5	3	2	1	6
1	4	3	5	2	7	6	8	9
6	5	7	9	8	4	1	3	2
9	2	8	1	3	6	4	5	7

4 7

4	2	7	8	1	5	6	3	9
8	5	9	4	3	6	2	7	1
6	1	3	2	9	7	4	8	5
7	3	6	1	5	4	8	9	2
5	4	1	9	8	2	3	6	7
2	9	8	7	6	3	5	1	4
9	7	5	3	4	8	1	2	6
1	8	4	6	2	9	7	5	3
3	6	2	5	7	1	9	4	8

4 8

5	3	1	8	9	4	2	6	7
2	7	6	3	5	1	9	8	4
4	9	8	2	7	6	3	5	1
7	4	2	5	8	9	1	3	6
9	8	5	1	6	3	4	7	2
6	1	3	7	4	2	8	9	5
1	6	7	9	2	8	5	4	3
3	5	9	4	1	7	6	2	8
8	2	4	6	3	5	7	1	9

49

7	2	9	6	4	3	8	1	5
1	5	4	7	2	8	9	3	6
6	8	3	1	9	5	2	7	4
5	3	2	4	6	7	1	9	8
4	9	7	8	3	1	5	6	2
8	1	6	2	5	9	7	4	3
2	7	1	3	8	6	4	5	9
3	4	5	9	1	2	6	8	7
9	6	8	5	7	4	3	2	1

50

8	3	6	7	9	5	2	1	4
7	5	9	2	4	1	3	6	8
1	2	4	6	8	3	9	5	7
2	6	7	1	3	8	4	9	5
4	9	1	5	6	7	8	3	2
5	8	3	4	2	9	6	7	1
3	7	8	9	1	2	5	4	6
6	1	2	3	5	4	7	8	9
9	4	5	8	7	6	1	2	3

51

9	1	3	4	8	6	2	7	5
4	7	5	2	1	3	9	6	8
2	6	8	9	5	7	1	4	3
5	2	1	6	9	4	8	3	7
3	4	6	1	7	8	5	2	9
7	8	9	3	2	5	6	1	4
8	3	2	7	6	9	4	5	1
6	5	4	8	3	1	7	9	2
1	9	7	5	4	2	3	8	6

52

8	3	4	2	7	5	6	1	9
7	5	2	1	9	6	8	3	4
9	6	1	8	4	3	5	7	2
2	8	9	4	6	7	3	5	1
5	1	7	9	3	8	4	2	6
6	4	3	5	1	2	9	8	7
4	2	8	7	5	9	1	6	3
3	9	5	6	2	1	7	4	8
1	7	6	3	8	4	2	9	5

53

3	5	6	1	7	4	9	2	8
7	4	9	8	5	2	1	6	3
1	8	2	9	6	3	5	4	7
6	2	4	7	1	8	3	5	9
9	7	8	5	3	6	2	1	4
5	3	1	2	4	9	7	8	6
8	1	3	4	2	7	6	9	5
4	6	5	3	9	1	8	7	2
2	9	7	6	8	5	4	3	1

54

1	6	9	4	3	8	5	2	7
7	3	4	5	2	1	6	8	9
8	2	5	9	6	7	4	1	3
4	8	1	2	7	3	9	6	5
2	7	3	6	9	5	8	4	1
9	5	6	1	8	4	7	3	2
5	1	8	3	4	9	2	7	6
6	9	7	8	1	2	3	5	4
3	4	2	7	5	6	1	9	8

55

3	2	8	1	4	7	5	6	9
6	1	5	8	3	9	2	7	4
4	7	9	6	5	2	1	3	8
1	3	7	2	8	4	9	5	6
9	6	4	3	7	5	8	2	1
8	5	2	9	6	1	7	4	3
5	8	1	4	2	6	3	9	7
7	4	3	5	9	8	6	1	2
2	9	6	7	1	3	4	8	5

56

3	2	4	6	7	9	8	5	1
8	5	1	2	4	3	9	6	7
7	9	6	1	5	8	3	4	2
4	6	2	5	8	1	7	3	9
5	8	9	3	2	7	6	1	4
1	3	7	4	9	6	2	8	5
6	7	8	9	1	5	4	2	3
2	1	3	7	6	4	5	9	8
9	4	5	8	3	2	1	7	6

5 7

2	6	1	3	5	4	7	8	9
3	4	7	9	2	8	5	6	1
8	9	5	6	1	7	3	2	4
5	3	2	4	6	1	9	7	8
1	8	4	2	7	9	6	3	5
9	7	6	5	8	3	4	1	2
4	5	8	1	3	6	2	9	7
6	1	9	7	4	2	8	5	3
7	2	3	8	9	5	1	4	6

5 8

5	2	1	7	8	6	9	4	3
9	7	3	4	1	2	8	6	5
6	8	4	9	3	5	7	1	2
4	6	8	5	7	3	2	9	1
3	5	9	6	2	1	4	8	7
2	1	7	8	4	9	5	3	6
7	3	2	1	9	4	6	5	8
8	9	6	3	5	7	1	2	4
1	4	5	2	6	8	3	7	9

5 9

4	9	2	7	5	3	6	8	1
5	3	1	6	8	4	9	7	2
7	8	6	2	1	9	3	4	5
6	4	8	9	7	5	2	1	3
3	5	9	4	2	1	7	6	8
1	2	7	3	6	8	4	5	9
9	6	5	1	3	7	8	2	4
2	1	4	8	9	6	5	3	7
8	7	3	5	4	2	1	9	6

6 0

5	6	2	3	1	9	7	8	4
4	7	1	5	8	6	9	3	2
8	9	3	4	7	2	6	1	5
2	4	7	8	6	5	3	9	1
6	8	9	1	2	3	5	4	7
1	3	5	9	4	7	2	6	8
3	5	8	7	9	4	1	2	6
7	2	4	6	3	1	8	5	9
9	1	6	2	5	8	4	7	3

6 1

2	6	3	7	9	4	8	5	1
4	1	7	5	6	8	9	2	3
9	8	5	3	1	2	4	7	6
3	2	4	8	7	9	1	6	5
8	7	6	1	2	5	3	4	9
5	9	1	6	4	3	7	8	2
1	5	8	2	3	7	6	9	4
7	3	9	4	5	6	2	1	8
6	4	2	9	8	1	5	3	7

6 2

6	3	8	9	4	1	7	5	2
1	9	4	7	5	2	8	6	3
5	7	2	3	6	8	9	4	1
2	4	3	8	1	7	6	9	5
7	5	6	2	9	4	1	3	8
8	1	9	5	3	6	4	2	7
4	8	5	6	7	3	2	1	9
3	2	1	4	8	9	5	7	6
9	6	7	1	2	5	3	8	4

6 3

4	6	8	3	9	1	5	7	2
1	7	3	2	6	5	4	9	8
2	5	9	7	8	4	1	3	6
7	8	4	5	3	9	2	6	1
6	9	5	1	4	2	7	8	3
3	1	2	8	7	6	9	5	4
8	2	1	9	5	3	6	4	7
5	4	7	6	1	8	3	2	9
9	3	6	4	2	7	8	1	5

6 4

2	4	1	3	6	5	8	7	9
7	6	3	9	8	1	4	5	2
9	5	8	7	4	2	1	3	6
3	1	4	2	5	7	9	6	8
6	9	7	8	1	3	2	4	5
8	2	5	6	9	4	3	1	7
1	7	6	4	2	8	5	9	3
4	3	2	5	7	9	6	8	1
5	8	9	1	3	6	7	2	4

65

3	8	4	1	5	6	9	2	7
6	7	2	4	9	3	8	5	1
5	9	1	2	7	8	6	4	3
2	6	9	8	1	7	5	3	4
4	3	5	9	6	2	7	1	8
7	1	8	3	4	5	2	6	9
8	5	3	7	2	1	4	9	6
1	4	6	5	8	9	3	7	2
9	2	7	6	3	4	1	8	5

66

4	5	2	7	8	3	1	6	9
3	1	7	9	6	5	8	4	2
6	8	9	1	4	2	7	3	5
2	9	4	5	1	6	3	8	7
5	6	1	3	7	8	9	2	4
7	3	8	4	2	9	6	5	1
8	4	6	2	9	7	5	1	3
1	7	5	6	3	4	2	9	8
9	2	3	8	5	1	4	7	6

67

1	2	4	5	3	6	9	7	8
7	3	5	9	1	8	4	6	2
8	9	6	7	2	4	5	1	3
5	1	3	4	6	2	7	8	9
4	6	7	1	8	9	3	2	5
2	8	9	3	5	7	6	4	1
9	4	1	2	7	3	8	5	6
6	7	2	8	9	5	1	3	4
3	5	8	6	4	1	2	9	7

68

1	3	9	4	7	5	8	2	6
6	8	4	1	2	9	3	5	7
5	2	7	3	8	6	9	4	1
4	7	6	9	3	1	5	8	2
3	9	1	8	5	2	6	7	4
2	5	8	6	4	7	1	9	3
9	6	5	2	1	4	7	3	8
8	1	2	7	9	3	4	6	5
7	4	3	5	6	8	2	1	9

69

6	5	8	4	2	7	3	9	1
1	7	4	9	3	8	6	2	5
2	3	9	6	1	5	7	4	8
7	8	1	2	5	3	4	6	9
4	9	2	1	8	6	5	3	7
5	6	3	7	4	9	1	8	2
3	4	7	8	9	1	2	5	6
8	2	6	5	7	4	9	1	3
9	1	5	3	6	2	8	7	4

70

7	4	1	8	9	5	3	6	2
2	5	6	1	4	3	9	7	8
3	9	8	2	6	7	5	4	1
5	6	3	4	7	2	1	8	9
8	2	9	6	5	1	4	3	7
4	1	7	9	3	8	2	5	6
1	3	4	7	2	6	8	9	5
9	7	2	5	8	4	6	1	3
6	8	5	3	1	9	7	2	4

71

6	9	3	1	2	7	5	8	4
7	5	1	4	8	3	2	9	6
8	4	2	5	9	6	1	7	3
3	2	4	6	7	5	8	1	9
9	7	6	8	1	4	3	5	2
1	8	5	2	3	9	6	4	7
2	3	9	7	5	1	4	6	8
5	6	8	9	4	2	7	3	1
4	1	7	3	6	8	9	2	5

72

7	6	2	4	5	1	9	8	3
5	3	9	6	8	7	2	1	4
4	1	8	3	9	2	6	7	5
2	7	4	1	3	9	5	6	8
8	9	3	7	6	5	1	4	2
1	5	6	8	2	4	7	3	9
9	8	1	5	7	3	4	2	6
3	4	5	2	1	6	8	9	7
6	2	7	9	4	8	3	5	1

73

8	3	7	5	1	2	6	9	4
5	6	9	3	7	4	8	2	1
2	1	4	6	8	9	3	5	7
4	7	5	1	3	6	9	8	2
6	2	8	4	9	5	7	1	3
3	9	1	8	2	7	5	4	6
1	4	6	7	5	8	2	3	9
7	5	2	9	4	3	1	6	8
9	8	3	2	6	1	4	7	5

74

6	2	5	8	3	7	1	4	9
3	7	9	4	6	1	2	8	5
1	8	4	9	2	5	6	7	3
7	4	6	1	5	9	3	2	8
2	3	8	6	7	4	9	5	1
9	5	1	3	8	2	4	6	7
8	1	7	2	4	3	5	9	6
4	6	3	5	9	8	7	1	2
5	9	2	7	1	6	8	3	4

75

2	4	3	9	8	1	7	6	5
9	1	8	6	5	7	2	4	3
5	6	7	4	3	2	1	9	8
1	9	6	5	2	8	4	3	7
3	8	4	7	9	6	5	2	1
7	2	5	1	4	3	9	8	6
6	7	9	8	1	4	3	5	2
4	3	1	2	6	5	8	7	9
8	5	2	3	7	9	6	1	4

76

7	6	9	1	4	2	3	5	8
2	1	4	3	5	8	7	9	6
5	3	8	9	7	6	1	4	2
8	9	3	4	1	7	2	6	5
4	5	7	6	2	9	8	3	1
1	2	6	5	8	3	9	7	4
9	7	2	8	6	5	4	1	3
6	8	1	7	3	4	5	2	9
3	4	5	2	9	1	6	8	7

77

7	8	3	5	2	4	1	6	9
2	1	5	9	7	6	3	8	4
4	9	6	3	8	1	7	2	5
1	2	8	7	6	5	9	4	3
5	3	9	2	4	8	6	1	7
6	7	4	1	9	3	8	5	2
9	6	2	8	5	7	4	3	1
3	4	7	6	1	2	5	9	8
8	5	1	4	3	9	2	7	6

78

2	4	5	1	6	9	7	8	3
3	9	8	2	7	5	1	4	6
6	7	1	3	8	4	5	9	2
4	1	6	9	3	8	2	7	5
7	8	3	4	5	2	6	1	9
5	2	9	7	1	6	8	3	4
8	5	7	6	4	3	9	2	1
9	6	4	8	2	1	3	5	7
1	3	2	5	9	7	4	6	8

79

8	9	7	2	5	4	1	3	6
5	2	4	6	1	3	9	8	7
3	1	6	9	8	7	5	2	4
9	3	8	5	6	1	7	4	2
4	7	1	3	2	9	8	6	5
6	5	2	4	7	8	3	1	9
7	4	3	8	9	6	2	5	1
1	8	5	7	4	2	6	9	3
2	6	9	1	3	5	4	7	8

80

2	1	6	4	5	9	3	7	8
9	7	3	8	2	1	6	5	4
8	4	5	3	6	7	2	9	1
3	5	4	1	7	2	9	8	6
7	2	9	6	8	4	5	1	3
1	6	8	9	3	5	4	2	7
5	3	7	2	4	8	1	6	9
6	9	2	7	1	3	8	4	5
4	8	1	5	9	6	7	3	2

8-1

7	3	9	1	8	4	5	2	6
8	5	1	2	6	3	4	9	7
2	6	4	7	5	9	8	3	1
9	1	8	6	4	7	2	5	3
6	2	3	5	9	1	7	4	8
4	7	5	8	3	2	6	1	9
5	4	6	3	1	8	9	7	2
1	8	2	9	7	5	3	6	4
3	9	7	4	2	6	1	8	5

8-2

3	5	7	2	1	9	8	6	4
1	2	6	5	8	4	7	3	9
9	8	4	7	3	6	5	1	2
6	3	2	8	4	7	1	9	5
8	9	5	1	2	3	4	7	6
4	7	1	9	6	5	2	8	3
5	1	3	4	9	8	6	2	7
7	6	8	3	5	2	9	4	1
2	4	9	6	7	1	3	5	8

8-3

8	9	4	7	5	1	6	3	2
1	6	7	2	3	8	9	5	4
3	5	2	4	6	9	8	7	1
2	1	9	5	4	7	3	6	8
7	4	6	8	1	3	5	2	9
5	8	3	9	2	6	4	1	7
4	3	8	1	7	5	2	9	6
9	7	5	6	8	2	1	4	3
6	2	1	3	9	4	7	8	5

8-4

9	1	2	3	6	8	7	5	4
4	3	5	9	7	2	8	1	6
7	8	6	4	1	5	2	9	3
3	9	1	5	2	4	6	7	8
2	4	8	6	9	7	5	3	1
6	5	7	8	3	1	4	2	9
1	2	9	7	4	6	3	8	5
8	7	4	1	5	3	9	6	2
5	6	3	2	8	9	1	4	7

8-5

6	3	9	4	7	1	2	8	5
1	7	8	2	6	5	4	3	9
4	2	5	8	3	9	7	6	1
9	6	3	5	2	8	1	4	7
2	4	7	6	1	3	9	5	8
8	5	1	7	9	4	3	2	6
5	8	2	9	4	7	6	1	3
7	1	6	3	8	2	5	9	4
3	9	4	1	5	6	8	7	2

8-6

4	6	3	7	5	8	2	9	1
1	7	2	4	9	6	5	3	8
5	8	9	3	1	2	7	4	6
9	5	7	1	2	4	6	8	3
8	2	4	5	6	3	1	7	9
6	3	1	8	7	9	4	2	5
7	1	8	9	4	5	3	6	2
2	9	5	6	3	7	8	1	4
3	4	6	2	8	1	9	5	7

8-7

3	2	5	9	8	4	6	7	1
6	4	8	2	1	7	5	9	3
9	7	1	6	5	3	2	8	4
5	9	4	7	2	1	8	3	6
7	1	3	5	6	8	9	4	2
2	8	6	3	4	9	7	1	5
1	6	9	4	7	5	3	2	8
8	5	7	1	3	2	4	6	9
4	3	2	8	9	6	1	5	7

8-8

7	9	4	2	3	5	8	6	1
6	1	5	4	9	8	2	3	7
3	8	2	1	6	7	5	4	9
4	5	6	3	7	2	1	9	8
2	7	9	6	8	1	4	5	3
8	3	1	9	5	4	6	7	2
1	6	8	7	4	3	9	2	5
9	2	3	5	1	6	7	8	4
5	4	7	8	2	9	3	1	6

8/9

4	8	3	9	5	6	1	2	7
9	5	6	2	1	7	3	4	8
7	1	2	8	4	3	9	6	5
5	6	7	4	9	1	2	8	3
3	2	8	7	6	5	4	1	9
1	4	9	3	8	2	5	7	6
8	3	5	6	2	4	7	9	1
2	9	1	5	7	8	6	3	4
6	7	4	1	3	9	8	5	2

9/0

7	2	9	3	5	6	4	1	8
8	6	5	4	7	1	3	9	2
4	3	1	2	8	9	7	6	5
5	9	7	6	1	8	2	3	4
6	1	3	7	4	2	8	5	9
2	8	4	5	9	3	6	7	1
3	4	8	1	6	5	9	2	7
1	7	6	9	2	4	5	8	3
9	5	2	8	3	7	1	4	6

9/1

8	4	5	6	7	2	9	3	1
6	3	7	9	4	1	2	5	8
2	9	1	8	3	5	7	6	4
4	2	8	3	1	7	6	9	5
9	1	6	2	5	8	3	4	7
5	7	3	4	9	6	8	1	2
7	6	9	5	8	4	1	2	3
1	5	2	7	6	3	4	8	9
3	8	4	1	2	9	5	7	6

9/2

8	4	9	7	5	1	2	6	3
3	1	5	4	2	6	9	8	7
7	6	2	8	3	9	5	1	4
1	9	4	2	6	5	3	7	8
6	3	8	1	9	7	4	2	5
2	5	7	3	8	4	1	9	6
9	7	1	5	4	8	6	3	2
4	2	6	9	7	3	8	5	1
5	8	3	6	1	2	7	4	9

9/3

7	5	9	1	3	8	4	6	2
8	6	2	5	9	4	7	1	3
4	1	3	7	2	6	9	8	5
9	4	8	3	1	5	2	7	6
2	3	1	6	4	7	8	5	9
6	7	5	2	8	9	1	3	4
1	2	7	9	5	3	6	4	8
3	8	6	4	7	2	5	9	1
5	9	4	8	6	1	3	2	7

9/4

3	4	8	5	1	9	7	2	6
1	6	7	8	2	3	5	4	9
2	5	9	4	6	7	1	8	3
5	9	6	1	7	2	8	3	4
8	3	1	6	9	4	2	7	5
4	7	2	3	5	8	6	9	1
9	1	3	2	8	6	4	5	7
6	8	4	7	3	5	9	1	2
7	2	5	9	4	1	3	6	8

9/5

5	3	9	2	6	4	8	7	1
8	2	7	1	5	3	9	4	6
4	6	1	9	8	7	2	3	5
3	4	2	6	1	9	7	5	8
9	8	5	7	3	2	6	1	4
7	1	6	5	4	8	3	9	2
1	7	8	3	2	5	4	6	9
6	9	4	8	7	1	5	2	3
2	5	3	4	9	6	1	8	7

9/6

8	9	2	5	7	6	4	1	3
4	5	3	9	1	8	7	6	2
1	6	7	4	2	3	5	8	9
6	3	8	1	9	5	2	4	7
9	2	1	7	8	4	3	5	6
7	4	5	3	6	2	8	9	1
2	7	6	8	4	9	1	3	5
5	1	4	6	3	7	9	2	8
3	8	9	2	5	1	6	7	4

97

1	9	8	5	3	4	6	7	2
2	6	3	8	9	7	4	5	1
5	7	4	2	1	6	3	8	9
3	1	5	9	4	8	2	6	7
9	8	6	3	7	2	1	4	5
7	4	2	1	6	5	8	9	3
8	5	1	4	2	9	7	3	6
6	2	9	7	8	3	5	1	4
4	3	7	6	5	1	9	2	8

98

2	5	3	9	6	8	7	4	1
1	9	6	7	2	4	3	5	8
7	4	8	3	5	1	2	9	6
8	6	2	5	4	3	1	7	9
5	7	1	6	8	9	4	3	2
4	3	9	2	1	7	6	8	5
6	8	4	1	3	5	9	2	7
3	1	7	8	9	2	5	6	4
9	2	5	4	7	6	8	1	3

99

9	3	7	6	1	2	5	8	4
4	6	5	8	9	7	3	1	2
8	1	2	4	3	5	7	9	6
6	4	8	2	5	9	1	7	3
3	2	1	7	8	6	4	5	9
7	5	9	3	4	1	2	6	8
5	8	4	9	7	3	6	2	1
1	9	6	5	2	4	8	3	7
2	7	3	1	6	8	9	4	5

100

1	3	2	5	6	4	9	7	8
9	8	6	2	3	7	1	5	4
4	7	5	8	9	1	6	3	2
6	5	4	9	1	8	7	2	3
8	9	1	7	2	3	4	6	5
7	2	3	4	5	6	8	9	1
5	6	9	1	8	2	3	4	7
3	4	8	6	7	5	2	1	9
2	1	7	3	4	9	5	8	6

101

7	4	1	8	5	3	6	2	9
8	6	5	9	7	2	1	3	4
9	2	3	6	4	1	7	8	5
1	7	6	4	3	5	8	9	2
5	9	2	1	6	8	4	7	3
3	8	4	2	9	7	5	1	6
4	1	9	3	8	6	2	5	7
2	3	7	5	1	4	9	6	8
6	5	8	7	2	9	3	4	1

102

5	1	3	7	4	2	6	8	9
9	7	4	8	1	6	2	3	5
2	6	8	9	5	3	7	1	4
1	9	5	3	8	7	4	6	2
7	3	2	6	9	4	1	5	8
4	8	6	5	2	1	9	7	3
6	4	9	1	3	8	5	2	7
3	2	7	4	6	5	8	9	1
8	5	1	2	7	9	3	4	6

103

5	1	6	4	8	3	2	9	7
9	3	7	2	6	1	4	8	5
4	8	2	7	9	5	1	6	3
6	7	9	3	1	8	5	2	4
3	4	1	9	5	2	8	7	6
2	5	8	6	7	4	3	1	9
7	2	3	8	4	6	9	5	1
8	9	5	1	3	7	6	4	2
1	6	4	5	2	9	7	3	8

104

2	6	1	3	9	7	8	5	4
5	9	8	1	4	2	3	6	7
4	7	3	8	6	5	2	9	1
9	3	6	7	8	4	1	2	5
7	2	5	9	1	3	6	4	8
8	1	4	2	5	6	7	3	9
3	5	9	6	7	8	4	1	2
6	4	7	5	2	1	9	8	3
1	8	2	4	3	9	5	7	6

105

7	4	1	9	2	5	8	6	3
2	6	8	7	3	1	5	9	4
9	5	3	4	8	6	7	2	1
5	2	7	6	9	3	4	1	8
8	9	4	1	7	2	3	5	6
1	3	6	8	5	4	9	7	2
6	8	2	5	4	7	1	3	9
4	1	5	3	6	9	2	8	7
3	7	9	2	1	8	6	4	5

106

7	2	1	3	5	4	6	9	8
4	5	8	9	7	6	1	3	2
9	3	6	1	8	2	7	5	4
2	1	7	4	6	3	9	8	5
5	8	4	7	9	1	3	2	6
6	9	3	8	2	5	4	1	7
8	6	9	5	1	7	2	4	3
3	7	5	2	4	9	8	6	1
1	4	2	6	3	8	5	7	9

107

8	7	1	3	5	6	4	2	9
2	5	4	7	9	8	3	6	1
3	6	9	1	4	2	7	8	5
6	4	2	5	7	1	8	9	3
1	8	3	4	6	9	2	5	7
5	9	7	8	2	3	1	4	6
4	2	5	6	3	7	9	1	8
9	3	8	2	1	5	6	7	4
7	1	6	9	8	4	5	3	2

108

8	9	4	2	1	6	3	7	5
6	5	7	4	3	8	2	1	9
2	1	3	7	5	9	6	4	8
7	2	8	5	6	3	4	9	1
1	3	9	8	4	7	5	2	6
4	6	5	1	9	2	8	3	7
9	4	2	6	8	1	7	5	3
5	8	1	3	7	4	9	6	2
3	7	6	9	2	5	1	8	4

109

4	6	5	2	8	9	3	7	1
2	9	7	3	1	6	5	8	4
3	8	1	5	7	4	2	9	6
6	7	3	4	2	8	1	5	9
1	4	8	6	9	5	7	2	3
9	5	2	1	3	7	4	6	8
7	3	9	8	4	2	6	1	5
8	1	6	7	5	3	9	4	2
5	2	4	9	6	1	8	3	7

110

3	8	7	1	9	6	2	5	4
9	5	2	4	8	7	6	1	3
1	4	6	3	2	5	9	7	8
2	9	3	7	6	1	8	4	5
4	6	5	8	3	9	7	2	1
8	7	1	5	4	2	3	6	9
6	1	9	2	5	3	4	8	7
7	2	4	9	1	8	5	3	6
5	3	8	6	7	4	1	9	2

111

7	9	4	2	5	1	8	6	3
6	5	2	3	9	8	1	7	4
8	3	1	7	4	6	2	5	9
1	4	7	8	6	2	3	9	5
9	8	5	4	3	7	6	2	1
2	6	3	5	1	9	4	8	7
4	7	8	1	2	5	9	3	6
3	2	6	9	7	4	5	1	8
5	1	9	6	8	3	7	4	2

112

5	8	9	4	7	1	6	3	2
6	7	1	5	3	2	8	9	4
4	2	3	6	9	8	5	7	1
2	3	7	8	4	5	1	6	9
1	6	5	7	2	9	3	4	8
9	4	8	3	1	6	7	2	5
3	5	2	1	6	4	9	8	7
7	1	4	9	8	3	2	5	6
8	9	6	2	5	7	4	1	3

113

5	1	7	4	3	9	2	8	6
8	3	6	2	5	1	7	4	9
9	4	2	6	7	8	5	1	3
3	5	9	1	8	6	4	7	2
6	8	4	7	2	5	3	9	1
2	7	1	9	4	3	6	5	8
1	9	5	3	6	4	8	2	7
7	6	8	5	9	2	1	3	4
4	2	3	8	1	7	9	6	5

114

7	4	6	9	1	8	5	2	3
2	9	1	6	3	5	8	7	4
8	3	5	4	7	2	1	9	6
5	6	4	7	8	3	2	1	9
9	8	3	1	2	4	7	6	5
1	7	2	5	6	9	4	3	8
4	1	9	3	5	7	6	8	2
3	2	7	8	4	6	9	5	1
6	5	8	2	9	1	3	4	7

115

3	8	4	6	1	5	2	9	7
7	6	2	9	3	4	1	8	5
1	9	5	2	7	8	6	4	3
5	7	1	8	6	3	4	2	9
8	3	9	7	4	2	5	1	6
4	2	6	1	5	9	3	7	8
9	5	8	3	2	1	7	6	4
6	1	3	4	9	7	8	5	2
2	4	7	5	8	6	9	3	1

116

7	8	4	5	3	6	9	2	1
1	5	2	7	9	8	3	4	6
9	3	6	4	1	2	5	7	8
4	1	5	3	8	9	7	6	2
3	6	9	1	2	7	8	5	4
2	7	8	6	5	4	1	3	9
6	9	1	2	7	3	4	8	5
5	4	3	8	6	1	2	9	7
8	2	7	9	4	5	6	1	3

117

4	3	5	8	1	2	7	9	6
7	6	2	9	5	3	1	4	8
1	8	9	6	7	4	5	3	2
3	2	8	7	4	9	6	5	1
6	7	4	1	2	5	9	8	3
9	5	1	3	6	8	4	2	7
2	1	3	5	9	6	8	7	4
8	9	7	4	3	1	2	6	5
5	4	6	2	8	7	3	1	9

118

8	4	7	6	3	1	2	9	5
9	3	6	2	5	4	8	1	7
1	2	5	9	8	7	4	3	6
7	8	4	5	1	3	9	6	2
2	6	3	7	4	9	5	8	1
5	1	9	8	6	2	7	4	3
4	7	2	3	9	6	1	5	8
3	9	8	1	7	5	6	2	4
6	5	1	4	2	8	3	7	9

119

2	4	8	7	1	6	9	5	3
5	6	3	2	9	8	4	1	7
7	9	1	3	4	5	6	2	8
9	2	7	1	5	3	8	6	4
6	8	5	4	7	2	3	9	1
1	3	4	8	6	9	5	7	2
3	5	2	6	8	1	7	4	9
4	1	6	9	3	7	2	8	5
8	7	9	5	2	4	1	3	6

120

6	1	2	8	9	4	5	7	3
7	5	3	1	2	6	8	4	9
8	9	4	5	3	7	2	1	6
9	6	5	3	4	8	1	2	7
2	4	1	9	7	5	3	6	8
3	7	8	6	1	2	9	5	4
1	2	6	4	8	3	7	9	5
4	8	7	2	5	9	6	3	1
5	3	9	7	6	1	4	8	2

121

5	8	4	6	2	1	9	3	7
2	9	1	3	7	8	5	6	4
3	7	6	5	9	4	8	1	2
9	1	7	4	8	6	2	5	3
8	3	5	2	1	7	6	4	9
6	4	2	9	3	5	7	8	1
4	2	3	8	6	9	1	7	5
1	5	8	7	4	2	3	9	6
7	6	9	1	5	3	4	2	8

122

3	2	5	9	1	7	8	4	6
8	4	7	3	5	6	2	9	1
9	6	1	4	8	2	3	7	5
1	8	2	6	9	4	5	3	7
5	7	4	8	2	3	1	6	9
6	3	9	1	7	5	4	8	2
2	9	3	5	6	8	7	1	4
7	1	8	2	4	9	6	5	3
4	5	6	7	3	1	9	2	8

123

6	7	4	1	3	2	5	9	8
8	5	9	4	6	7	1	2	3
3	1	2	9	5	8	4	6	7
2	8	1	3	4	6	7	5	9
7	3	5	2	8	9	6	4	1
4	9	6	7	1	5	8	3	2
5	2	7	6	9	1	3	8	4
1	4	8	5	2	3	9	7	6
9	6	3	8	7	4	2	1	5

124

9	2	8	5	3	4	7	1	6
7	6	3	9	8	1	5	4	2
4	5	1	6	7	2	3	9	8
1	9	5	8	4	3	2	6	7
2	3	7	1	5	6	4	8	9
6	8	4	2	9	7	1	3	5
8	4	2	3	6	5	9	7	1
3	1	9	7	2	8	6	5	4
5	7	6	4	1	9	8	2	3

125

8	9	7	4	2	1	5	3	6
1	4	6	5	3	7	2	9	8
3	2	5	9	8	6	4	7	1
7	8	9	6	4	5	1	2	3
6	1	3	8	9	2	7	5	4
2	5	4	7	1	3	6	8	9
9	7	1	3	5	4	8	6	2
5	3	2	1	6	8	9	4	7
4	6	8	2	7	9	3	1	5

126

8	9	4	3	1	2	5	6	7
1	5	7	9	8	6	2	3	4
3	6	2	4	7	5	9	8	1
5	7	1	8	4	9	3	2	6
2	8	3	6	5	7	1	4	9
6	4	9	1	2	3	7	5	8
4	2	5	7	9	8	6	1	3
7	1	6	2	3	4	8	9	5
9	3	8	5	6	1	4	7	2

127

3	4	1	9	7	2	6	5	8
2	7	9	5	8	6	4	1	3
6	8	5	1	4	3	7	2	9
8	6	7	4	1	9	2	3	5
9	1	3	2	5	7	8	4	6
5	2	4	3	6	8	1	9	7
1	9	6	7	2	5	3	8	4
4	3	8	6	9	1	5	7	2
7	5	2	8	3	4	9	6	1

128

8	9	5	3	1	7	6	2	4
4	3	6	9	2	5	8	7	1
2	1	7	8	6	4	5	9	3
7	8	4	6	9	3	1	5	2
9	5	2	1	4	8	7	3	6
3	6	1	5	7	2	4	8	9
5	2	9	4	8	1	3	6	7
1	7	3	2	5	6	9	4	8
6	4	8	7	3	9	2	1	5

129

3	1	8	9	2	4	6	5	7
6	5	9	1	3	7	8	2	4
2	7	4	8	5	6	3	1	9
5	2	3	4	8	9	7	6	1
4	9	7	3	6	1	5	8	2
8	6	1	2	7	5	9	4	3
1	8	5	7	9	2	4	3	6
9	4	6	5	1	3	2	7	8
7	3	2	6	4	8	1	9	5

130

2	9	7	6	4	1	3	5	8
8	5	3	9	7	2	1	6	4
6	1	4	5	8	3	9	7	2
7	2	9	3	5	6	4	8	1
1	6	8	4	9	7	5	2	3
3	4	5	1	2	8	6	9	7
9	7	1	2	3	5	8	4	6
5	8	6	7	1	4	2	3	9
4	3	2	8	6	9	7	1	5

131

7	6	8	4	9	1	3	5	2
1	3	4	8	5	2	6	9	7
9	2	5	3	6	7	1	4	8
5	8	6	1	2	9	4	7	3
4	1	2	6	7	3	9	8	5
3	9	7	5	4	8	2	1	6
8	7	9	2	1	6	5	3	4
2	4	3	9	8	5	7	6	1
6	5	1	7	3	4	8	2	9

132

5	9	1	7	4	6	8	2	3
3	4	8	2	5	1	6	7	9
6	7	2	8	9	3	4	5	1
8	6	4	1	3	2	7	9	5
7	2	3	5	8	9	1	4	6
9	1	5	4	6	7	3	8	2
1	8	9	3	2	4	5	6	7
2	5	7	6	1	8	9	3	4
4	3	6	9	7	5	2	1	8

133

3	5	2	1	4	6	7	9	8
9	6	4	7	8	2	5	3	1
7	8	1	9	5	3	6	4	2
5	1	7	4	3	8	9	2	6
2	4	6	5	7	9	1	8	3
8	9	3	2	6	1	4	5	7
1	7	8	3	9	4	2	6	5
6	2	9	8	1	5	3	7	4
4	3	5	6	2	7	8	1	9

134

5	7	9	4	1	2	3	8	6
2	1	4	6	8	3	5	9	7
3	8	6	7	9	5	2	1	4
4	2	3	5	7	1	8	6	9
8	6	5	3	4	9	1	7	2
1	9	7	2	6	8	4	5	3
6	3	1	9	5	4	7	2	8
7	4	8	1	2	6	9	3	5
9	5	2	8	3	7	6	4	1

135

6	9	3	1	2	8	4	7	5
2	8	4	7	9	5	1	3	6
1	5	7	4	6	3	8	2	9
5	3	1	6	7	9	2	8	4
4	2	9	8	5	1	7	6	3
8	7	6	3	4	2	5	9	1
3	6	2	5	8	4	9	1	7
7	4	8	9	1	6	3	5	2
9	1	5	2	3	7	6	4	8

136

5	4	8	7	6	1	2	9	3
1	7	3	4	2	9	6	8	5
6	2	9	3	5	8	4	7	1
7	6	2	1	8	4	3	5	9
9	3	4	5	7	2	8	1	6
8	1	5	9	3	6	7	4	2
3	5	1	6	4	7	9	2	8
4	8	6	2	9	5	1	3	7
2	9	7	8	1	3	5	6	4

137

5	7	1	4	3	8	9	2	6
2	8	9	6	1	7	3	4	5
4	3	6	5	9	2	8	7	1
6	2	3	8	7	1	4	5	9
9	5	7	3	4	6	1	8	2
8	1	4	2	5	9	7	6	3
3	4	8	9	6	5	2	1	7
1	9	5	7	2	4	6	3	8
7	6	2	1	8	3	5	9	4

138

2	5	3	8	6	1	4	9	7
9	7	6	4	3	2	8	1	5
1	8	4	7	5	9	6	2	3
7	9	8	2	4	3	1	5	6
3	4	1	6	8	5	2	7	9
6	2	5	9	1	7	3	4	8
5	6	2	3	7	4	9	8	1
8	1	9	5	2	6	7	3	4
4	3	7	1	9	8	5	6	2

139

8	3	6	1	7	5	9	2	4
5	9	1	3	2	4	8	7	6
7	2	4	6	8	9	5	1	3
2	6	5	8	4	3	7	9	1
9	1	3	7	5	6	2	4	8
4	7	8	2	9	1	3	6	5
6	4	7	9	3	8	1	5	2
1	8	9	5	6	2	4	3	7
3	5	2	4	1	7	6	8	9

140

8	5	9	6	4	1	7	2	3
4	2	3	9	5	7	6	1	8
1	6	7	3	8	2	9	5	4
6	4	2	7	3	5	8	9	1
3	7	5	1	9	8	4	6	2
9	8	1	2	6	4	5	3	7
2	1	6	8	7	9	3	4	5
7	9	4	5	1	3	2	8	6
5	3	8	4	2	6	1	7	9

141

6	3	7	2	4	1	8	5	9
1	5	2	8	9	7	6	4	3
9	4	8	3	6	5	7	2	1
8	6	5	1	2	4	9	3	7
3	1	9	5	7	8	4	6	2
7	2	4	6	3	9	5	1	8
2	7	3	9	5	6	1	8	4
5	9	1	4	8	2	3	7	6
4	8	6	7	1	3	2	9	5

142

3	6	9	2	1	5	4	7	8
5	7	2	8	9	4	6	1	3
4	8	1	6	3	7	5	2	9
8	3	4	9	7	6	1	5	2
2	9	7	5	4	1	8	3	6
6	1	5	3	8	2	7	9	4
1	4	3	7	2	8	9	6	5
9	5	8	1	6	3	2	4	7
7	2	6	4	5	9	3	8	1

143

3	6	1	2	5	8	7	9	4
4	8	2	9	3	7	6	1	5
9	7	5	1	4	6	3	2	8
8	2	3	4	6	5	1	7	9
1	4	6	7	9	3	8	5	2
7	5	9	8	1	2	4	6	3
2	9	4	6	8	1	5	3	7
5	1	7	3	2	4	9	8	6
6	3	8	5	7	9	2	4	1

144

3	6	2	4	1	8	9	5	7
1	8	4	5	7	9	3	6	2
5	9	7	2	3	6	1	8	4
9	2	3	7	8	4	6	1	5
4	7	1	6	9	5	8	2	3
8	5	6	1	2	3	4	7	9
7	4	8	3	6	2	5	9	1
6	1	5	9	4	7	2	3	8
2	3	9	8	5	1	7	4	6

145

2	3	9	7	4	5	6	1	8
5	6	1	9	8	3	4	2	7
8	7	4	1	2	6	5	3	9
7	1	3	8	5	2	9	4	6
4	2	5	6	9	7	3	8	1
6	9	8	4	3	1	2	7	5
9	4	7	3	6	8	1	5	2
1	5	6	2	7	4	8	9	3
3	8	2	5	1	9	7	6	4

146

2	5	8	1	4	3	6	9	7
9	4	7	8	2	6	1	3	5
1	6	3	5	7	9	4	8	2
4	7	5	2	9	1	3	6	8
6	3	9	4	5	8	7	2	1
8	2	1	6	3	7	9	5	4
3	8	4	9	1	2	5	7	6
5	9	6	7	8	4	2	1	3
7	1	2	3	6	5	8	4	9

147

2	9	8	5	6	4	1	3	7
3	6	5	7	9	1	4	2	8
7	1	4	2	8	3	9	5	6
5	2	6	9	3	7	8	1	4
1	8	3	6	4	5	7	9	2
4	7	9	8	1	2	5	6	3
6	3	7	1	5	8	2	4	9
8	4	1	3	2	9	6	7	5
9	5	2	4	7	6	3	8	1

148

5	9	4	7	8	2	3	1	6
6	7	3	5	4	1	9	2	8
8	2	1	9	6	3	7	4	5
7	4	6	1	5	8	2	3	9
1	3	9	6	2	7	8	5	4
2	8	5	4	3	9	1	6	7
4	1	2	8	7	6	5	9	3
3	5	7	2	9	4	6	8	1
9	6	8	3	1	5	4	7	2

149

3	7	9	6	5	4	2	1	8
5	2	4	9	1	8	3	7	6
6	8	1	2	7	3	9	5	4
1	4	7	8	3	2	6	9	5
9	5	2	1	6	7	8	4	3
8	3	6	5	4	9	1	2	7
4	6	3	7	2	1	5	8	9
7	1	8	3	9	5	4	6	2
2	9	5	4	8	6	7	3	1

150

3	5	2	8	7	9	1	6	4
1	8	6	3	4	5	7	2	9
4	9	7	1	6	2	5	3	8
6	4	3	2	5	1	8	9	7
8	7	1	4	9	3	6	5	2
5	2	9	6	8	7	3	4	1
7	1	4	5	2	6	9	8	3
9	6	8	7	3	4	2	1	5
2	3	5	9	1	8	4	7	6

151

7	1	2	6	9	8	4	3	5
9	8	4	3	5	1	2	6	7
5	6	3	2	7	4	8	1	9
1	3	6	4	2	5	7	9	8
4	2	7	9	8	3	6	5	1
8	9	5	1	6	7	3	2	4
6	7	1	8	3	9	5	4	2
2	5	9	7	4	6	1	8	3
3	4	8	5	1	2	9	7	6

152

2	9	5	4	8	1	3	7	6
1	6	7	9	5	3	8	4	2
8	3	4	6	7	2	1	5	9
3	4	6	7	2	9	5	8	1
5	2	8	3	1	6	7	9	4
7	1	9	5	4	8	6	2	3
4	8	3	2	6	7	9	1	5
9	5	1	8	3	4	2	6	7
6	7	2	1	9	5	4	3	8

153

7	9	8	4	3	5	6	2	1
6	2	1	7	8	9	5	3	4
4	5	3	2	1	6	7	9	8
1	7	4	3	9	2	8	5	6
9	8	2	6	5	7	4	1	3
5	3	6	1	4	8	9	7	2
3	6	7	5	2	4	1	8	9
2	4	9	8	7	1	3	6	5
8	1	5	9	6	3	2	4	7

154

6	7	4	2	9	3	8	1	5
1	5	3	8	7	6	2	4	9
9	8	2	1	4	5	6	3	7
4	1	5	6	2	7	3	9	8
7	2	9	4	3	8	1	5	6
8	3	6	9	5	1	7	2	4
3	9	8	5	6	2	4	7	1
2	4	1	7	8	9	5	6	3
5	6	7	3	1	4	9	8	2

155

1	9	8	4	2	3	6	7	5
6	5	7	8	1	9	2	4	3
3	2	4	6	5	7	9	8	1
2	7	6	3	8	4	1	5	9
8	1	5	7	9	2	3	6	4
4	3	9	5	6	1	8	2	7
9	8	1	2	4	5	7	3	6
7	4	2	1	3	6	5	9	8
5	6	3	9	7	8	4	1	2

156

8	5	7	2	3	6	9	4	1
2	1	6	4	8	9	3	5	7
9	4	3	5	1	7	8	2	6
1	9	2	6	5	3	7	8	4
3	6	8	7	2	4	1	9	5
4	7	5	1	9	8	2	6	3
6	2	9	3	4	1	5	7	8
7	8	1	9	6	5	4	3	2
5	3	4	8	7	2	6	1	9

157

8	5	2	7	9	1	6	4	3
4	9	6	5	8	3	2	1	7
1	3	7	2	4	6	8	9	5
3	6	9	1	2	7	5	8	4
5	2	1	8	3	4	9	7	6
7	8	4	6	5	9	3	2	1
9	1	8	3	7	5	4	6	2
2	7	3	4	6	8	1	5	9
6	4	5	9	1	2	7	3	8

158

4	3	2	5	9	1	8	6	7
1	8	5	7	6	2	9	3	4
7	9	6	8	3	4	5	1	2
9	7	3	1	5	8	2	4	6
6	2	8	3	4	9	7	5	1
5	1	4	2	7	6	3	8	9
8	6	7	4	2	3	1	9	5
2	4	1	9	8	5	6	7	3
3	5	9	6	1	7	4	2	8

159

6	5	7	1	4	9	8	3	2
4	1	3	6	8	2	7	9	5
9	2	8	7	3	5	1	6	4
1	4	6	2	5	7	3	8	9
2	3	9	8	6	1	5	4	7
8	7	5	4	9	3	6	2	1
7	9	2	3	1	8	4	5	6
5	8	4	9	7	6	2	1	3
3	6	1	5	2	4	9	7	8

160

2	4	3	5	6	9	1	8	7
1	5	6	7	3	8	2	9	4
7	8	9	2	4	1	6	3	5
5	2	7	9	1	6	3	4	8
3	1	4	8	5	2	9	7	6
9	6	8	4	7	3	5	1	2
6	7	2	1	9	4	8	5	3
4	3	1	6	8	5	7	2	9
8	9	5	3	2	7	4	6	1

161

6	5	7	9	8	4	3	1	2
3	8	1	2	6	5	7	9	4
2	4	9	3	7	1	6	5	8
4	6	8	1	9	7	2	3	5
7	1	5	6	2	3	8	4	9
9	3	2	4	5	8	1	6	7
8	9	3	7	4	6	5	2	1
1	7	4	5	3	2	9	8	6
5	2	6	8	1	9	4	7	3

162

9	5	1	6	4	3	7	8	2
2	4	8	5	1	7	3	6	9
7	6	3	2	8	9	4	5	1
6	2	5	3	9	4	1	7	8
8	3	7	1	5	2	6	9	4
1	9	4	7	6	8	5	2	3
5	7	2	9	3	1	8	4	6
4	1	6	8	2	5	9	3	7
3	8	9	4	7	6	2	1	5

163

4	9	1	5	2	3	6	8	7
2	6	3	7	9	8	4	5	1
7	8	5	6	1	4	2	3	9
1	3	2	4	6	5	9	7	8
6	4	9	1	8	7	3	2	5
5	7	8	9	3	2	1	4	6
8	2	6	3	7	1	5	9	4
3	1	4	8	5	9	7	6	2
9	5	7	2	4	6	8	1	3

164

4	3	9	5	8	6	7	1	2
8	2	7	3	4	1	5	6	9
1	5	6	2	9	7	8	3	4
3	1	4	6	7	2	9	8	5
9	8	2	1	5	4	6	7	3
6	7	5	8	3	9	4	2	1
7	6	3	9	1	5	2	4	8
5	4	8	7	2	3	1	9	6
2	9	1	4	6	8	3	5	7

165

7	4	3	1	8	6	9	2	5
2	5	6	3	9	7	1	8	4
8	9	1	2	5	4	6	7	3
1	7	8	4	6	2	3	5	9
9	3	2	5	7	1	8	4	6
5	6	4	9	3	8	7	1	2
6	2	5	8	1	3	4	9	7
3	1	9	7	4	5	2	6	8
4	8	7	6	2	9	5	3	1

166

1	4	8	5	9	3	7	2	6
5	6	2	8	7	4	3	9	1
9	3	7	1	2	6	5	8	4
4	8	1	7	6	5	9	3	2
6	2	5	3	8	9	1	4	7
7	9	3	2	4	1	6	5	8
8	5	4	9	1	7	2	6	3
2	7	9	6	3	8	4	1	5
3	1	6	4	5	2	8	7	9

167

2	7	5	6	1	3	4	8	9
6	8	4	5	2	9	1	3	7
9	3	1	4	7	8	2	6	5
3	5	8	9	4	6	7	1	2
1	9	6	2	3	7	8	5	4
4	2	7	1	8	5	3	9	6
8	1	9	7	5	2	6	4	3
7	6	3	8	9	4	5	2	1
5	4	2	3	6	1	9	7	8

168

7	2	4	3	5	8	9	1	6
3	6	9	2	1	4	5	7	8
5	1	8	7	6	9	4	3	2
9	4	3	5	8	7	2	6	1
2	7	6	1	4	3	8	5	9
8	5	1	6	9	2	7	4	3
1	9	7	8	3	5	6	2	4
6	8	2	4	7	1	3	9	5
4	3	5	9	2	6	1	8	7

169

9	6	1	8	2	4	3	7	5
3	4	7	1	5	6	2	9	8
5	2	8	3	9	7	6	4	1
1	3	9	4	8	2	5	6	7
4	5	2	7	6	1	9	8	3
8	7	6	9	3	5	4	1	2
2	9	4	5	1	8	7	3	6
7	1	5	6	4	3	8	2	9
6	8	3	2	7	9	1	5	4

170

5	7	3	9	1	2	4	8	6
2	8	4	6	3	5	9	7	1
1	6	9	8	7	4	2	3	5
3	9	5	2	4	1	7	6	8
8	1	7	3	9	6	5	4	2
6	4	2	7	5	8	3	1	9
7	3	6	5	8	9	1	2	4
4	5	8	1	2	7	6	9	3
9	2	1	4	6	3	8	5	7

171

1	4	2	8	3	7	5	6	9
3	6	5	9	1	4	7	2	8
9	8	7	2	5	6	1	3	4
2	3	1	5	4	8	9	7	6
4	5	6	7	9	1	2	8	3
7	9	8	6	2	3	4	5	1
8	1	9	3	7	2	6	4	5
6	2	4	1	8	5	3	9	7
5	7	3	4	6	9	8	1	2

172

3	1	6	5	2	9	8	7	4
8	5	4	1	6	7	2	9	3
7	9	2	4	8	3	1	6	5
9	4	1	6	5	2	7	3	8
5	3	7	8	9	4	6	2	1
6	2	8	7	3	1	5	4	9
2	8	5	9	4	6	3	1	7
1	6	9	3	7	8	4	5	2
4	7	3	2	1	5	9	8	6

173

9	2	4	3	6	5	7	8	1
5	3	8	1	7	2	6	9	4
6	1	7	8	9	4	3	2	5
1	9	2	6	5	8	4	3	7
4	7	5	9	2	3	8	1	6
8	6	3	4	1	7	9	5	2
3	4	6	5	8	1	2	7	9
2	8	1	7	4	9	5	6	3
7	5	9	2	3	6	1	4	8

174

6	5	9	7	3	4	8	1	2
3	1	8	2	6	5	9	7	4
4	2	7	8	1	9	6	5	3
8	4	3	1	7	6	2	9	5
2	7	5	4	9	3	1	8	6
9	6	1	5	2	8	3	4	7
5	3	2	9	4	1	7	6	8
7	9	4	6	8	2	5	3	1
1	8	6	3	5	7	4	2	9

175

4	5	3	1	6	7	2	8	9
6	7	9	8	3	2	4	1	5
2	8	1	5	9	4	6	3	7
3	9	6	2	7	1	8	5	4
7	1	5	4	8	6	9	2	3
8	4	2	3	5	9	7	6	1
5	2	7	9	1	8	3	4	6
9	3	8	6	4	5	1	7	2
1	6	4	7	2	3	5	9	8

176

5	1	6	7	9	8	3	2	4
7	8	4	2	3	6	1	5	9
3	2	9	5	1	4	7	6	8
9	5	1	8	7	3	6	4	2
4	6	3	1	2	9	5	8	7
8	7	2	4	6	5	9	3	1
6	4	7	3	8	1	2	9	5
1	3	5	9	4	2	8	7	6
2	9	8	6	5	7	4	1	3

177

1	5	3	4	7	6	9	2	8
9	2	8	5	3	1	7	6	4
6	7	4	9	2	8	3	1	5
2	9	5	6	4	3	8	7	1
8	3	1	7	9	5	2	4	6
7	4	6	8	1	2	5	9	3
4	8	9	3	6	7	1	5	2
5	1	7	2	8	4	6	3	9
3	6	2	1	5	9	4	8	7

178

4	7	3	5	1	2	8	9	6
6	9	2	8	7	4	1	3	5
8	5	1	9	6	3	7	2	4
3	1	8	4	9	5	6	7	2
5	4	9	7	2	6	3	8	1
2	6	7	1	3	8	5	4	9
7	2	5	6	8	9	4	1	3
9	8	4	3	5	1	2	6	7
1	3	6	2	4	7	9	5	8

179

8	4	7	6	5	1	2	9	3
2	6	1	7	9	3	8	5	4
5	3	9	4	8	2	1	7	6
3	2	5	8	7	4	6	1	9
1	9	8	3	6	5	7	4	2
4	7	6	2	1	9	5	3	8
6	5	3	9	2	7	4	8	1
7	8	4	1	3	6	9	2	5
9	1	2	5	4	8	3	6	7

180

4	8	3	1	6	5	7	2	9
7	2	6	3	9	4	1	5	8
9	5	1	8	2	7	3	4	6
2	3	4	6	1	8	5	9	7
8	6	7	4	5	9	2	3	1
5	1	9	2	7	3	6	8	4
3	4	5	7	8	6	9	1	2
1	7	8	9	3	2	4	6	5
6	9	2	5	4	1	8	7	3

181

9	7	1	5	6	4	8	2	3
4	6	3	2	8	7	5	1	9
2	8	5	3	9	1	7	4	6
1	2	4	9	5	6	3	8	7
6	3	7	1	2	8	4	9	5
8	5	9	4	7	3	2	6	1
7	1	2	6	4	5	9	3	8
5	9	6	8	3	2	1	7	4
3	4	8	7	1	9	6	5	2

182

5	3	9	4	2	1	7	6	8
7	2	1	6	5	8	4	9	3
6	4	8	7	9	3	1	5	2
4	9	7	1	8	2	6	3	5
1	6	5	9	3	4	8	2	7
2	8	3	5	6	7	9	4	1
9	1	4	2	7	5	3	8	6
8	7	2	3	4	6	5	1	9
3	5	6	8	1	9	2	7	4

183

7	5	3	1	2	8	6	9	4
6	1	8	4	5	9	7	3	2
9	4	2	3	6	7	5	1	8
8	6	5	2	7	3	1	4	9
4	3	9	6	8	1	2	7	5
1	2	7	5	9	4	3	8	6
5	7	4	8	3	6	9	2	1
2	9	1	7	4	5	8	6	3
3	8	6	9	1	2	4	5	7

184

5	6	8	7	4	3	2	1	9
9	7	3	2	1	5	6	4	8
1	2	4	8	6	9	5	3	7
3	9	2	1	5	7	8	6	4
6	8	7	4	3	2	9	5	1
4	5	1	6	9	8	3	7	2
8	1	5	3	2	4	7	9	6
2	4	9	5	7	6	1	8	3
7	3	6	9	8	1	4	2	5

185

7	3	5	6	8	1	9	4	2
1	9	2	4	7	5	6	8	3
4	6	8	9	2	3	5	1	7
9	1	7	3	5	6	8	2	4
2	5	3	8	4	9	7	6	1
6	8	4	2	1	7	3	9	5
5	4	6	7	9	2	1	3	8
8	7	9	1	3	4	2	5	6
3	2	1	5	6	8	4	7	9

186

3	7	1	8	5	6	4	2	9
6	4	2	3	1	9	8	5	7
5	8	9	4	7	2	1	3	6
1	5	6	7	2	3	9	8	4
8	3	7	1	9	4	2	6	5
9	2	4	5	6	8	3	7	1
4	6	5	2	3	1	7	9	8
2	9	8	6	4	7	5	1	3
7	1	3	9	8	5	6	4	2

187

4	9	1	3	2	7	6	8	5
6	8	5	1	4	9	7	3	2
7	3	2	6	8	5	4	1	9
3	4	9	5	1	8	2	7	6
2	6	8	7	9	3	5	4	1
1	5	7	4	6	2	8	9	3
9	7	3	8	5	6	1	2	4
5	2	4	9	7	1	3	6	8
8	1	6	2	3	4	9	5	7

188

2	5	8	6	9	1	4	3	7
9	7	1	3	8	4	6	2	5
3	6	4	7	5	2	8	9	1
4	3	6	9	1	7	5	8	2
8	9	5	2	4	6	7	1	3
7	1	2	5	3	8	9	6	4
6	2	9	4	7	3	1	5	8
5	8	7	1	2	9	3	4	6
1	4	3	8	6	5	2	7	9

189

2	9	6	1	7	5	4	8	3
4	7	5	2	8	3	6	1	9
3	8	1	9	4	6	7	2	5
6	1	7	3	9	8	2	5	4
8	5	2	4	1	7	3	9	6
9	3	4	6	5	2	8	7	1
7	2	3	5	6	9	1	4	8
1	6	9	8	2	4	5	3	7
5	4	8	7	3	1	9	6	2

190

7	9	3	4	6	1	5	2	8
5	8	4	2	7	9	3	6	1
2	6	1	5	8	3	4	9	7
3	7	6	9	5	4	1	8	2
9	1	8	3	2	6	7	5	4
4	5	2	7	1	8	6	3	9
8	3	7	1	9	5	2	4	6
1	4	9	6	3	2	8	7	5
6	2	5	8	4	7	9	1	3

191

5	4	8	7	2	1	9	3	6
1	9	6	3	4	5	8	7	2
7	3	2	9	6	8	4	5	1
3	2	7	4	8	9	6	1	5
8	6	4	5	1	7	2	9	3
9	5	1	6	3	2	7	4	8
6	7	5	8	9	3	1	2	4
4	1	3	2	7	6	5	8	9
2	8	9	1	5	4	3	6	7

192

5	7	3	8	1	6	4	2	9
6	4	1	2	5	9	3	7	8
9	2	8	7	3	4	1	5	6
1	3	7	6	9	5	8	4	2
4	6	2	1	8	3	7	9	5
8	5	9	4	2	7	6	1	3
7	9	5	3	4	8	2	6	1
2	8	4	5	6	1	9	3	7
3	1	6	9	7	2	5	8	4

193

6	8	2	3	1	9	5	4	7
7	1	5	6	8	4	3	2	9
4	3	9	5	2	7	8	6	1
3	4	1	7	6	5	9	8	2
8	2	6	1	9	3	4	7	5
5	9	7	8	4	2	1	3	6
1	6	4	9	7	8	2	5	3
9	5	8	2	3	6	7	1	4
2	7	3	4	5	1	6	9	8

194

6	7	8	3	2	1	5	4	9
4	5	1	9	7	8	3	2	6
2	9	3	6	4	5	7	1	8
9	3	4	8	1	2	6	7	5
7	1	6	5	9	3	4	8	2
5	8	2	4	6	7	1	9	3
1	6	5	7	8	9	2	3	4
8	4	7	2	3	6	9	5	1
3	2	9	1	5	4	8	6	7

195

1	2	9	7	6	3	5	4	8
3	6	7	8	4	5	1	2	9
5	8	4	9	2	1	7	6	3
2	1	8	6	9	4	3	7	5
7	4	3	1	5	8	2	9	6
6	9	5	3	7	2	8	1	4
4	5	1	2	8	9	6	3	7
9	3	6	5	1	7	4	8	2
8	7	2	4	3	6	9	5	1

196

9	3	1	5	4	8	7	6	2
8	4	5	2	7	6	9	1	3
6	2	7	1	3	9	5	4	8
4	9	2	8	5	1	6	3	7
3	1	6	7	9	4	2	8	5
7	5	8	3	6	2	1	9	4
1	6	3	4	2	7	8	5	9
5	7	9	6	8	3	4	2	1
2	8	4	9	1	5	3	7	6

197

5	6	2	1	4	8	9	3	7
3	8	9	6	5	7	2	4	1
1	4	7	2	3	9	5	6	8
2	5	1	8	7	4	3	9	6
7	3	8	5	9	6	1	2	4
6	9	4	3	2	1	8	7	5
9	2	6	4	1	5	7	8	3
8	1	3	7	6	2	4	5	9
4	7	5	9	8	3	6	1	2

198

2	6	4	1	5	9	8	3	7
3	5	9	8	4	7	2	1	6
7	8	1	2	6	3	4	9	5
4	1	5	9	2	6	7	8	3
9	7	3	5	1	8	6	2	4
6	2	8	7	3	4	9	5	1
1	9	2	6	7	5	3	4	8
8	4	6	3	9	1	5	7	2
5	3	7	4	8	2	1	6	9

199

7	1	8	4	9	3	6	5	2
9	2	4	5	6	8	1	3	7
3	5	6	7	2	1	9	4	8
4	6	7	2	8	5	3	1	9
2	9	3	6	1	4	7	8	5
5	8	1	3	7	9	4	2	6
6	3	2	1	5	7	8	9	4
8	4	5	9	3	6	2	7	1
1	7	9	8	4	2	5	6	3

200

8	6	9	2	3	7	4	1	5
3	1	2	6	4	5	8	7	9
4	7	5	8	1	9	6	2	3
5	2	6	7	9	3	1	4	8
7	4	3	1	8	2	5	9	6
1	9	8	5	6	4	2	3	7
9	5	7	4	2	8	3	6	1
6	3	4	9	5	1	7	8	2
2	8	1	3	7	6	9	5	4

201

6	3	2	4	1	8	9	5	7
1	7	4	2	5	9	3	6	8
9	8	5	3	7	6	4	2	1
4	9	6	8	3	2	7	1	5
5	2	7	1	9	4	6	8	3
3	1	8	5	6	7	2	9	4
8	4	3	9	2	5	1	7	6
2	6	1	7	8	3	5	4	9
7	5	9	6	4	1	8	3	2

202

4	7	1	6	3	8	2	5	9
9	2	3	4	1	5	6	8	7
6	8	5	2	7	9	4	3	1
2	4	9	1	5	7	8	6	3
8	1	6	3	9	2	7	4	5
3	5	7	8	4	6	1	9	2
7	6	2	5	8	3	9	1	4
1	3	8	9	2	4	5	7	6
5	9	4	7	6	1	3	2	8

203

6	8	5	1	3	9	2	4	7
3	1	4	2	7	8	6	9	5
2	7	9	6	4	5	3	1	8
5	3	6	7	8	4	9	2	1
8	2	7	9	1	3	4	5	6
4	9	1	5	2	6	7	8	3
7	4	8	3	9	1	5	6	2
1	6	2	4	5	7	8	3	9
9	5	3	8	6	2	1	7	4

204

1	3	6	9	4	5	7	2	8
4	5	8	2	7	6	3	9	1
9	2	7	3	1	8	6	5	4
5	8	9	4	6	7	1	3	2
2	6	4	5	3	1	8	7	9
7	1	3	8	2	9	5	4	6
6	7	2	1	9	3	4	8	5
3	9	5	6	8	4	2	1	7
8	4	1	7	5	2	9	6	3

205

8	9	4	6	1	2	7	3	5
2	1	6	7	3	5	9	8	4
5	7	3	4	9	8	1	6	2
7	6	9	5	2	1	3	4	8
3	4	5	8	6	7	2	9	1
1	8	2	3	4	9	6	5	7
6	2	8	1	5	3	4	7	9
9	3	7	2	8	4	5	1	6
4	5	1	9	7	6	8	2	3

206

3	4	1	8	6	5	9	2	7
7	6	9	3	2	1	8	5	4
8	2	5	9	4	7	1	6	3
5	1	8	6	7	3	4	9	2
9	7	6	4	8	2	5	3	1
2	3	4	1	5	9	7	8	6
4	5	7	2	9	6	3	1	8
1	8	2	5	3	4	6	7	9
6	9	3	7	1	8	2	4	5

207

1	9	7	5	4	2	6	8	3
8	4	2	6	3	7	5	1	9
5	3	6	9	8	1	4	2	7
7	6	8	4	1	9	2	3	5
3	2	9	7	6	5	8	4	1
4	1	5	8	2	3	7	9	6
2	7	3	1	5	4	9	6	8
9	8	4	3	7	6	1	5	2
6	5	1	2	9	8	3	7	4

208

3	8	7	6	9	5	2	1	4
4	9	2	8	1	3	6	5	7
1	5	6	2	4	7	8	3	9
6	7	9	4	2	1	3	8	5
8	1	4	5	3	6	9	7	2
5	2	3	7	8	9	1	4	6
7	3	1	9	5	2	4	6	8
9	6	8	3	7	4	5	2	1
2	4	5	1	6	8	7	9	3

209

3	6	4	7	9	1	8	2	5
8	5	7	6	2	3	1	4	9
1	2	9	5	8	4	3	7	6
9	3	5	2	6	7	4	1	8
2	8	1	4	3	5	9	6	7
4	7	6	8	1	9	2	5	3
7	9	2	1	5	8	6	3	4
5	1	3	9	4	6	7	8	2
6	4	8	3	7	2	5	9	1

210

5	1	3	2	4	9	8	6	7
6	4	2	8	7	1	9	3	5
8	7	9	5	6	3	2	1	4
2	9	4	7	3	8	6	5	1
3	8	6	1	5	4	7	2	9
1	5	7	6	9	2	4	8	3
7	3	8	9	2	5	1	4	6
9	2	5	4	1	6	3	7	8
4	6	1	3	8	7	5	9	2

211

3	2	4	8	1	5	6	9	7
5	7	8	4	9	6	1	2	3
9	1	6	3	2	7	5	4	8
6	9	3	1	8	2	4	7	5
7	8	1	5	6	4	2	3	9
2	4	5	7	3	9	8	1	6
4	5	9	2	7	8	3	6	1
8	3	7	6	4	1	9	5	2
1	6	2	9	5	3	7	8	4

212

9	5	4	8	1	6	2	3	7
6	3	7	9	4	2	1	8	5
2	8	1	7	5	3	4	6	9
8	1	9	2	6	7	3	5	4
7	4	5	3	9	1	8	2	6
3	6	2	5	8	4	9	7	1
1	7	6	4	2	8	5	9	3
4	9	8	6	3	5	7	1	2
5	2	3	1	7	9	6	4	8

213

9	8	6	3	2	1	7	4	5
5	3	7	9	4	8	1	6	2
2	1	4	6	7	5	3	8	9
7	6	2	4	5	9	8	3	1
3	9	8	2	1	7	4	5	6
1	4	5	8	3	6	2	9	7
8	5	3	7	9	2	6	1	4
4	7	1	5	6	3	9	2	8
6	2	9	1	8	4	5	7	3

214

3	1	5	2	7	4	6	8	9
2	9	7	6	8	5	1	3	4
6	4	8	3	9	1	5	7	2
8	2	3	1	6	9	7	4	5
4	5	9	7	2	8	3	6	1
1	7	6	5	4	3	2	9	8
5	6	4	9	3	2	8	1	7
7	8	1	4	5	6	9	2	3
9	3	2	8	1	7	4	5	6

215

6	1	7	4	3	2	8	9	5
9	8	2	6	7	5	3	1	4
5	3	4	1	9	8	2	6	7
4	6	1	3	5	7	9	8	2
2	9	3	8	4	6	7	5	1
8	7	5	9	2	1	6	4	3
3	2	9	5	6	4	1	7	8
1	4	6	7	8	3	5	2	9
7	5	8	2	1	9	4	3	6

216

7	5	8	6	2	1	4	9	3
1	3	4	8	9	7	2	6	5
6	2	9	3	4	5	1	8	7
5	9	1	4	8	2	7	3	6
3	7	2	5	1	6	8	4	9
4	8	6	7	3	9	5	2	1
2	1	3	9	7	4	6	5	8
8	4	5	1	6	3	9	7	2
9	6	7	2	5	8	3	1	4

217

8	2	3	9	7	1	4	6	5
4	7	6	3	5	8	9	1	2
9	1	5	4	2	6	8	3	7
6	9	4	5	1	2	3	7	8
5	8	7	6	9	3	2	4	1
1	3	2	7	8	4	6	5	9
3	5	8	2	6	7	1	9	4
2	6	9	1	4	5	7	8	3
7	4	1	8	3	9	5	2	6

218

7	2	9	4	5	3	6	8	1
5	6	1	8	9	2	7	3	4
4	3	8	1	6	7	9	2	5
8	1	4	6	7	5	2	9	3
2	7	5	3	4	9	1	6	8
6	9	3	2	8	1	4	5	7
9	5	6	7	1	8	3	4	2
3	4	7	5	2	6	8	1	9
1	8	2	9	3	4	5	7	6

219

6	3	1	5	4	7	9	8	2
4	8	2	3	6	9	5	1	7
9	5	7	2	1	8	6	4	3
2	1	3	9	7	4	8	6	5
7	6	8	1	5	3	2	9	4
5	9	4	6	8	2	7	3	1
8	7	5	4	3	6	1	2	9
1	4	9	8	2	5	3	7	6
3	2	6	7	9	1	4	5	8

220

8	7	5	2	6	1	3	9	4
6	9	3	8	7	4	5	1	2
2	4	1	5	9	3	7	8	6
9	5	4	7	2	8	1	6	3
3	2	6	1	4	9	8	5	7
7	1	8	3	5	6	2	4	9
1	6	2	9	3	5	4	7	8
4	8	7	6	1	2	9	3	5
5	3	9	4	8	7	6	2	1

221

1	4	6	9	5	3	7	8	2
9	8	5	7	1	2	4	6	3
7	3	2	6	8	4	5	9	1
5	2	8	1	9	6	3	4	7
3	6	9	2	4	7	8	1	5
4	1	7	8	3	5	6	2	9
2	5	1	4	7	8	9	3	6
8	9	3	5	6	1	2	7	4
6	7	4	3	2	9	1	5	8

222

9	2	8	6	1	5	3	7	4
3	7	5	4	2	9	6	1	8
6	1	4	8	3	7	5	2	9
4	5	6	3	9	2	7	8	1
8	9	1	5	7	6	2	4	3
2	3	7	1	4	8	9	5	6
1	4	9	7	5	3	8	6	2
7	8	2	9	6	1	4	3	5
5	6	3	2	8	4	1	9	7

223

9	6	5	4	8	3	7	1	2
8	7	4	9	2	1	5	3	6
2	1	3	6	7	5	8	4	9
1	2	8	7	6	4	9	5	3
3	9	7	1	5	2	4	6	8
5	4	6	3	9	8	1	2	7
6	8	1	2	4	9	3	7	5
7	3	9	5	1	6	2	8	4
4	5	2	8	3	7	6	9	1

224

3	5	7	8	6	1	9	2	4
4	1	6	5	9	2	8	3	7
8	9	2	4	3	7	5	6	1
6	7	4	9	2	5	3	1	8
5	2	8	1	7	3	6	4	9
1	3	9	6	4	8	2	7	5
2	4	3	7	8	9	1	5	6
9	6	1	3	5	4	7	8	2
7	8	5	2	1	6	4	9	3

225

2	3	5	4	9	8	7	1	6
8	7	6	3	1	2	9	5	4
1	4	9	7	5	6	3	2	8
4	9	1	6	8	5	2	7	3
7	8	3	9	2	4	1	6	5
6	5	2	1	7	3	4	8	9
9	2	4	5	6	7	8	3	1
3	6	8	2	4	1	5	9	7
5	1	7	8	3	9	6	4	2

226

9	5	3	1	8	7	2	6	4
8	7	2	4	9	6	1	5	3
4	6	1	5	3	2	7	8	9
7	2	4	9	1	8	5	3	6
6	9	5	2	7	3	8	4	1
1	3	8	6	5	4	9	2	7
2	4	9	7	6	5	3	1	8
5	8	7	3	4	1	6	9	2
3	1	6	8	2	9	4	7	5

227

4	2	5	1	9	6	3	7	8
1	3	6	2	7	8	5	9	4
9	7	8	5	3	4	2	6	1
2	1	3	4	8	7	6	5	9
6	4	9	3	1	5	7	8	2
5	8	7	6	2	9	1	4	3
8	5	2	9	6	3	4	1	7
7	6	1	8	4	2	9	3	5
3	9	4	7	5	1	8	2	6

228

3	5	2	8	1	9	7	4	6
1	7	9	4	2	6	8	3	5
6	8	4	7	3	5	9	2	1
9	6	1	5	7	4	3	8	2
5	3	7	2	8	1	4	6	9
2	4	8	9	6	3	1	5	7
7	1	3	6	5	8	2	9	4
8	9	5	1	4	2	6	7	3
4	2	6	3	9	7	5	1	8

229

8	5	1	3	4	9	2	6	7
9	7	4	5	6	2	3	1	8
3	6	2	7	1	8	5	9	4
1	3	9	4	7	5	6	8	2
2	8	5	9	3	6	7	4	1
7	4	6	8	2	1	9	5	3
5	9	7	1	8	3	4	2	6
6	1	3	2	5	4	8	7	9
4	2	8	6	9	7	1	3	5

230

8	5	6	4	3	1	7	2	9
4	9	1	7	2	8	6	5	3
3	2	7	5	9	6	8	4	1
9	4	8	1	7	2	5	3	6
6	7	3	9	4	5	1	8	2
5	1	2	8	6	3	4	9	7
7	6	9	2	5	4	3	1	8
1	3	4	6	8	9	2	7	5
2	8	5	3	1	7	9	6	4

231

2	3	8	1	5	4	9	6	7
7	9	4	2	6	8	5	3	1
5	1	6	9	3	7	2	4	8
8	4	1	3	9	6	7	5	2
3	2	7	8	1	5	6	9	4
9	6	5	4	7	2	1	8	3
6	5	3	7	4	1	8	2	9
4	7	2	6	8	9	3	1	5
1	8	9	5	2	3	4	7	6

232

6	9	7	2	1	3	8	5	4
5	1	2	8	4	6	3	9	7
8	4	3	7	9	5	1	2	6
9	8	5	6	2	1	4	7	3
3	2	6	5	7	4	9	8	1
4	7	1	3	8	9	5	6	2
7	5	9	1	3	2	6	4	8
2	3	4	9	6	8	7	1	5
1	6	8	4	5	7	2	3	9

233

2	1	5	6	4	7	9	3	8
6	4	9	3	2	8	1	7	5
7	3	8	9	1	5	4	2	6
3	6	1	5	8	2	7	9	4
8	7	2	4	9	3	6	5	1
5	9	4	7	6	1	3	8	2
4	5	6	2	7	9	8	1	3
9	8	3	1	5	4	2	6	7
1	2	7	8	3	6	5	4	9

234

7	1	8	9	5	3	6	2	4
2	4	9	8	6	1	7	5	3
3	5	6	7	2	4	1	9	8
9	8	5	4	3	6	2	7	1
4	7	2	1	9	5	8	3	6
6	3	1	2	7	8	9	4	5
1	2	3	6	4	9	5	8	7
8	9	4	5	1	7	3	6	2
5	6	7	3	8	2	4	1	9

235

6	4	3	7	5	1	8	2	9
7	1	9	3	2	8	5	6	4
8	5	2	9	4	6	3	1	7
9	6	7	2	3	4	1	5	8
1	2	4	5	8	7	9	3	6
3	8	5	6	1	9	4	7	2
5	3	8	4	6	2	7	9	1
2	9	1	8	7	5	6	4	3
4	7	6	1	9	3	2	8	5

236

7	8	5	1	6	3	2	9	4
6	2	4	5	7	9	1	3	8
9	1	3	2	8	4	7	5	6
1	9	7	4	5	8	6	2	3
4	6	2	3	1	7	5	8	9
3	5	8	6	9	2	4	1	7
8	4	1	7	3	5	9	6	2
5	7	9	8	2	6	3	4	1
2	3	6	9	4	1	8	7	5

237

6	2	1	7	9	3	8	4	5
4	7	9	5	2	8	1	6	3
3	8	5	1	6	4	2	7	9
9	6	4	3	5	2	7	8	1
8	5	3	6	1	7	9	2	4
7	1	2	4	8	9	3	5	6
5	3	8	9	7	6	4	1	2
2	4	6	8	3	1	5	9	7
1	9	7	2	4	5	6	3	8

238

9	5	6	3	4	7	1	8	2
4	8	2	6	1	5	3	9	7
1	7	3	9	8	2	4	6	5
8	6	7	2	5	1	9	4	3
5	3	1	4	9	8	2	7	6
2	4	9	7	6	3	8	5	1
7	9	4	1	3	6	5	2	8
6	1	8	5	2	4	7	3	9
3	2	5	8	7	9	6	1	4

239

9	3	8	6	2	5	4	1	7
7	2	1	9	4	3	5	8	6
6	4	5	7	1	8	2	3	9
8	9	2	3	5	7	1	6	4
1	7	3	4	6	9	8	2	5
4	5	6	2	8	1	7	9	3
5	6	7	8	3	2	9	4	1
2	1	4	5	9	6	3	7	8
3	8	9	1	7	4	6	5	2

240

1	7	9	2	3	8	5	6	4
5	4	8	9	1	6	3	2	7
6	2	3	4	7	5	9	8	1
4	6	1	8	5	2	7	9	3
8	9	5	3	6	7	4	1	2
7	3	2	1	4	9	8	5	6
9	1	6	7	8	3	2	4	5
3	8	4	5	2	1	6	7	9
2	5	7	6	9	4	1	3	8

241

9	1	6	3	8	5	7	4	2
4	2	7	9	6	1	8	3	5
3	5	8	7	2	4	6	1	9
2	8	1	6	4	9	5	7	3
7	3	4	1	5	2	9	6	8
5	6	9	8	7	3	4	2	1
1	9	5	4	3	6	2	8	7
8	4	2	5	1	7	3	9	6
6	7	3	2	9	8	1	5	4

242

3	8	5	1	6	4	2	9	7
2	7	9	5	8	3	1	4	6
6	1	4	2	9	7	5	8	3
9	4	2	8	5	6	3	7	1
8	6	1	7	3	2	9	5	4
7	5	3	9	4	1	6	2	8
5	3	8	6	7	9	4	1	2
1	9	6	4	2	8	7	3	5
4	2	7	3	1	5	8	6	9

243

6	5	8	9	2	4	3	1	7
4	7	2	5	1	3	6	9	8
9	3	1	8	7	6	2	4	5
5	2	6	3	8	1	9	7	4
7	4	9	6	5	2	8	3	1
8	1	3	7	4	9	5	6	2
1	6	7	2	3	5	4	8	9
3	8	5	4	9	7	1	2	6
2	9	4	1	6	8	7	5	3

244

2	6	8	3	7	1	5	9	4
5	3	1	9	6	4	7	2	8
9	4	7	8	2	5	1	3	6
6	1	2	4	9	3	8	7	5
8	9	3	6	5	7	4	1	2
7	5	4	1	8	2	9	6	3
1	7	5	2	4	6	3	8	9
4	8	6	7	3	9	2	5	1
3	2	9	5	1	8	6	4	7

245

9	5	2	8	4	6	3	7	1
1	8	7	5	3	2	6	4	9
3	6	4	7	9	1	5	8	2
5	7	6	2	1	9	4	3	8
2	1	3	4	6	8	7	9	5
4	9	8	3	5	7	1	2	6
8	2	1	6	7	3	9	5	4
7	4	9	1	2	5	8	6	3
6	3	5	9	8	4	2	1	7

246

8	2	4	6	3	1	5	9	7
7	3	6	5	9	2	1	4	8
1	9	5	7	4	8	3	6	2
2	5	8	1	7	6	4	3	9
3	7	1	9	5	4	2	8	6
6	4	9	2	8	3	7	1	5
9	6	2	3	1	7	8	5	4
5	8	3	4	2	9	6	7	1
4	1	7	8	6	5	9	2	3

247

9	2	5	1	6	8	4	3	7
4	8	3	9	7	2	5	6	1
7	6	1	5	4	3	8	9	2
3	9	4	7	8	5	1	2	6
5	1	8	3	2	6	9	7	4
2	7	6	4	9	1	3	5	8
8	5	7	6	3	4	2	1	9
6	3	2	8	1	9	7	4	5
1	4	9	2	5	7	6	8	3

248

7	1	5	6	4	2	9	8	3
3	8	6	7	5	9	1	2	4
2	4	9	8	3	1	5	7	6
6	3	7	2	8	5	4	1	9
1	9	4	3	6	7	2	5	8
8	5	2	1	9	4	3	6	7
4	2	8	9	1	6	7	3	5
9	6	1	5	7	3	8	4	2
5	7	3	4	2	8	6	9	1

249

9	4	3	6	2	1	5	7	8
7	2	6	8	5	3	4	1	9
8	1	5	7	4	9	3	6	2
2	3	8	9	6	7	1	5	4
6	5	7	4	1	2	8	9	3
4	9	1	3	8	5	7	2	6
5	8	2	1	9	4	6	3	7
1	7	4	2	3	6	9	8	5
3	6	9	5	7	8	2	4	1

250

8	2	7	3	9	5	6	1	4
6	9	1	7	4	2	8	5	3
5	4	3	6	8	1	7	2	9
2	7	9	8	5	3	4	6	1
4	8	6	2	1	9	3	7	5
3	1	5	4	7	6	9	8	2
9	3	8	1	2	7	5	4	6
1	6	4	5	3	8	2	9	7
7	5	2	9	6	4	1	3	8

251

4	1	8	5	3	9	2	7	6
2	3	9	1	6	7	5	4	8
6	5	7	2	4	8	3	1	9
8	9	5	6	7	4	1	3	2
1	4	6	3	8	2	7	9	5
3	7	2	9	5	1	8	6	4
7	8	1	4	9	5	6	2	3
5	6	4	7	2	3	9	8	1
9	2	3	8	1	6	4	5	7

252

9	1	7	6	2	8	3	5	4
4	8	5	3	9	7	1	2	6
3	2	6	4	5	1	9	7	8
6	9	3	8	7	4	2	1	5
8	4	2	5	1	9	7	6	3
7	5	1	2	6	3	8	4	9
2	3	4	7	8	5	6	9	1
5	6	9	1	3	2	4	8	7
1	7	8	9	4	6	5	3	2

253

3	9	1	5	7	2	6	8	4
2	5	8	6	4	3	7	1	9
4	7	6	8	9	1	5	3	2
5	3	2	7	1	9	4	6	8
9	8	7	4	6	5	1	2	3
1	6	4	2	3	8	9	7	5
7	4	5	3	2	6	8	9	1
8	2	9	1	5	7	3	4	6
6	1	3	9	8	4	2	5	7

254

3	5	1	2	9	4	8	6	7
2	4	9	6	7	8	3	5	1
7	8	6	1	5	3	4	2	9
9	6	2	3	1	5	7	4	8
8	3	7	4	6	2	1	9	5
5	1	4	9	8	7	6	3	2
4	2	8	7	3	9	5	1	6
1	7	3	5	2	6	9	8	4
6	9	5	8	4	1	2	7	3

255

4	3	8	6	9	2	5	1	7
9	1	7	5	8	3	6	2	4
5	2	6	4	1	7	9	3	8
3	4	1	9	2	5	7	8	6
7	5	2	1	6	8	4	9	3
6	8	9	7	3	4	1	5	2
1	7	3	2	4	9	8	6	5
2	9	4	8	5	6	3	7	1
8	6	5	3	7	1	2	4	9

256

8	2	9	4	5	7	3	6	1
1	6	5	3	8	2	9	4	7
7	3	4	6	9	1	2	8	5
6	4	8	7	2	9	1	5	3
2	1	7	5	6	3	4	9	8
5	9	3	1	4	8	6	7	2
4	7	6	2	3	5	8	1	9
3	8	1	9	7	4	5	2	6
9	5	2	8	1	6	7	3	4

257

2	7	1	4	3	6	9	5	8
4	9	8	7	2	5	1	6	3
3	6	5	8	1	9	7	4	2
1	2	6	5	9	8	4	3	7
5	4	3	6	7	1	2	8	9
9	8	7	3	4	2	5	1	6
6	1	4	2	8	7	3	9	5
8	3	2	9	5	4	6	7	1
7	5	9	1	6	3	8	2	4

258

6	2	3	5	9	7	4	8	1
4	7	5	1	8	6	2	3	9
1	8	9	4	2	3	5	7	6
2	9	1	7	3	5	6	4	8
7	5	4	9	6	8	3	1	2
3	6	8	2	4	1	9	5	7
9	1	6	8	5	4	7	2	3
8	4	2	3	7	9	1	6	5
5	3	7	6	1	2	8	9	4

259

9	2	1	8	5	3	7	4	6
7	6	8	4	2	9	1	3	5
5	4	3	7	1	6	8	2	9
6	8	7	2	9	5	3	1	4
3	5	2	1	4	8	9	6	7
4	1	9	6	3	7	2	5	8
8	3	5	9	6	1	4	7	2
2	7	6	3	8	4	5	9	1
1	9	4	5	7	2	6	8	3

260

9	1	4	6	3	5	8	2	7
2	6	8	4	9	7	1	5	3
5	3	7	8	2	1	9	6	4
3	4	5	9	8	2	6	7	1
6	8	1	7	4	3	2	9	5
7	2	9	1	5	6	4	3	8
8	5	6	2	7	4	3	1	9
4	7	2	3	1	9	5	8	6
1	9	3	5	6	8	7	4	2

261

7	8	5	3	2	1	4	9	6
3	4	6	5	7	9	1	2	8
1	2	9	8	6	4	5	3	7
2	9	8	4	1	3	6	7	5
5	1	3	6	9	7	8	4	2
4	6	7	2	8	5	3	1	9
8	7	4	9	3	6	2	5	1
6	3	1	7	5	2	9	8	4
9	5	2	1	4	8	7	6	3

262

8	9	1	7	2	6	4	3	5
7	6	4	5	3	1	9	8	2
5	3	2	9	8	4	1	7	6
6	5	8	1	4	3	2	9	7
2	1	9	8	6	7	5	4	3
4	7	3	2	5	9	8	6	1
1	4	7	3	9	2	6	5	8
3	8	6	4	1	5	7	2	9
9	2	5	6	7	8	3	1	4

263

7	9	1	4	5	8	3	2	6
2	4	6	3	7	9	8	1	5
5	8	3	2	6	1	4	7	9
3	2	8	5	9	6	1	4	7
9	6	4	7	1	3	2	5	8
1	7	5	8	4	2	9	6	3
8	1	2	6	3	5	7	9	4
4	5	9	1	8	7	6	3	2
6	3	7	9	2	4	5	8	1

264

8	7	9	2	6	5	4	3	1
5	1	2	7	4	3	8	6	9
6	4	3	9	8	1	7	5	2
7	6	4	5	9	8	1	2	3
2	3	5	6	1	7	9	4	8
1	9	8	3	2	4	6	7	5
3	8	6	4	5	9	2	1	7
4	5	1	8	7	2	3	9	6
9	2	7	1	3	6	5	8	4

265

8	6	4	2	9	7	3	5	1
3	5	1	6	4	8	7	2	9
2	7	9	1	3	5	8	4	6
4	9	3	8	7	2	6	1	5
7	1	8	5	6	9	4	3	2
6	2	5	4	1	3	9	7	8
9	4	6	7	5	1	2	8	3
1	3	2	9	8	4	5	6	7
5	8	7	3	2	6	1	9	4

266

3	9	8	2	5	4	7	6	1
1	7	5	3	8	6	4	9	2
4	6	2	1	9	7	5	3	8
2	8	3	5	4	1	6	7	9
9	1	6	7	3	8	2	4	5
5	4	7	6	2	9	8	1	3
7	5	4	8	1	3	9	2	6
8	3	9	4	6	2	1	5	7
6	2	1	9	7	5	3	8	4

267

5	6	8	4	9	2	3	7	1
1	7	3	8	5	6	9	4	2
2	4	9	1	3	7	8	6	5
6	5	2	9	4	3	1	8	7
3	9	1	7	8	5	6	2	4
4	8	7	2	6	1	5	9	3
7	1	6	5	2	9	4	3	8
8	3	5	6	7	4	2	1	9
9	2	4	3	1	8	7	5	6

268

2	6	8	5	1	7	3	9	4
3	9	5	2	8	4	7	1	6
4	1	7	3	6	9	8	5	2
7	3	1	6	4	2	9	8	5
9	4	6	8	3	5	1	2	7
8	5	2	9	7	1	6	4	3
1	2	9	7	5	3	4	6	8
5	8	3	4	9	6	2	7	1
6	7	4	1	2	8	5	3	9

269

6	4	3	7	9	8	5	1	2
9	8	2	5	3	1	4	6	7
1	5	7	6	4	2	3	8	9
2	9	5	1	8	7	6	4	3
3	1	8	4	6	9	7	2	5
4	7	6	3	2	5	8	9	1
5	2	1	8	7	6	9	3	4
7	6	4	9	1	3	2	5	8
8	3	9	2	5	4	1	7	6

270

3	9	5	1	6	2	8	4	7
8	2	6	9	4	7	1	3	5
1	4	7	3	8	5	9	2	6
7	5	2	8	9	3	4	6	1
9	6	1	2	7	4	3	5	8
4	3	8	6	5	1	7	9	2
6	8	4	7	2	9	5	1	3
2	1	9	5	3	8	6	7	4
5	7	3	4	1	6	2	8	9

271

6	1	7	9	4	3	5	2	8
2	3	5	8	7	1	9	4	6
8	9	4	6	2	5	1	3	7
4	5	6	1	9	7	2	8	3
3	7	8	5	6	2	4	1	9
1	2	9	4	3	8	6	7	5
7	6	1	3	5	4	8	9	2
9	8	3	2	1	6	7	5	4
5	4	2	7	8	9	3	6	1

272

7	4	8	2	6	9	5	1	3
5	9	3	4	1	7	2	8	6
1	2	6	3	8	5	4	9	7
8	7	9	5	3	4	6	2	1
2	3	1	6	7	8	9	4	5
4	6	5	9	2	1	7	3	8
3	5	7	8	9	2	1	6	4
9	8	4	1	5	6	3	7	2
6	1	2	7	4	3	8	5	9

273

8	9	5	2	3	6	1	7	4
3	2	1	4	8	7	6	5	9
6	4	7	5	9	1	3	8	2
9	5	2	8	6	3	7	4	1
1	7	3	9	4	5	8	2	6
4	6	8	7	1	2	5	9	3
2	8	6	1	5	9	4	3	7
5	1	9	3	7	4	2	6	8
7	3	4	6	2	8	9	1	5

274

4	1	5	8	7	2	3	6	9
6	7	3	1	9	4	8	2	5
9	2	8	5	3	6	7	1	4
3	6	7	9	8	1	4	5	2
5	4	2	7	6	3	9	8	1
8	9	1	4	2	5	6	7	3
7	5	4	3	1	8	2	9	6
2	3	9	6	5	7	1	4	8
1	8	6	2	4	9	5	3	7

275

5	2	1	3	9	8	6	7	4
4	7	3	6	1	5	9	2	8
8	6	9	7	4	2	3	1	5
9	8	2	1	5	7	4	3	6
3	1	6	9	2	4	8	5	7
7	5	4	8	6	3	1	9	2
1	4	5	2	3	6	7	8	9
6	3	8	5	7	9	2	4	1
2	9	7	4	8	1	5	6	3

276

2	8	5	9	3	7	1	4	6
6	1	3	2	4	8	7	5	9
7	9	4	1	6	5	3	8	2
8	2	1	5	7	3	9	6	4
5	4	9	6	2	1	8	3	7
3	7	6	8	9	4	5	2	1
1	5	2	4	8	9	6	7	3
9	6	7	3	5	2	4	1	8
4	3	8	7	1	6	2	9	5

277

7	5	2	1	9	6	3	8	4
4	1	6	5	3	8	2	9	7
3	9	8	7	4	2	6	1	5
9	8	4	2	6	5	1	7	3
2	7	5	3	1	9	8	4	6
6	3	1	8	7	4	5	2	9
5	4	3	9	2	1	7	6	8
8	2	9	6	5	7	4	3	1
1	6	7	4	8	3	9	5	2

278

2	3	8	6	4	7	9	1	5
5	6	7	3	9	1	2	8	4
9	4	1	8	2	5	6	3	7
1	5	3	2	8	9	7	4	6
8	9	4	7	5	6	1	2	3
6	7	2	1	3	4	8	5	9
4	2	6	9	1	3	5	7	8
3	1	9	5	7	8	4	6	2
7	8	5	4	6	2	3	9	1

279

3	1	9	7	4	6	8	5	2
7	8	6	2	5	9	4	1	3
4	5	2	1	3	8	6	7	9
5	9	7	4	2	1	3	8	6
2	4	3	8	6	7	1	9	5
8	6	1	5	9	3	2	4	7
9	2	4	3	1	5	7	6	8
1	7	5	6	8	2	9	3	4
6	3	8	9	7	4	5	2	1

280

8	3	1	2	5	6	7	4	9
4	9	7	8	3	1	2	5	6
5	2	6	9	7	4	1	8	3
1	6	5	3	8	2	9	7	4
2	7	4	1	6	9	8	3	5
3	8	9	7	4	5	6	2	1
9	5	8	4	1	7	3	6	2
7	4	2	6	9	3	5	1	8
6	1	3	5	2	8	4	9	7

281

1	6	8	2	3	4	7	9	5
5	3	7	6	1	9	8	2	4
9	2	4	8	5	7	6	1	3
2	8	1	7	4	5	9	3	6
6	5	3	9	8	2	4	7	1
7	4	9	1	6	3	2	5	8
3	7	6	5	2	8	1	4	9
8	9	5	4	7	1	3	6	2
4	1	2	3	9	6	5	8	7

282

1	8	3	4	6	5	9	2	7
5	7	6	2	9	1	8	4	3
2	4	9	3	7	8	6	1	5
8	6	4	9	5	2	7	3	1
9	5	2	1	3	7	4	8	6
3	1	7	6	8	4	2	5	9
4	3	5	7	2	6	1	9	8
7	2	8	5	1	9	3	6	4
6	9	1	8	4	3	5	7	2

283

1	6	8	3	4	2	9	7	5
2	4	7	5	8	9	1	6	3
5	9	3	1	6	7	4	8	2
8	1	9	2	5	3	6	4	7
7	5	6	8	1	4	2	3	9
3	2	4	9	7	6	5	1	8
9	7	1	6	2	8	3	5	4
4	3	5	7	9	1	8	2	6
6	8	2	4	3	5	7	9	1

284

1	9	8	3	5	4	2	7	6
7	2	6	9	1	8	3	4	5
5	4	3	7	2	6	1	9	8
9	5	1	4	7	3	8	6	2
6	3	7	8	9	2	5	1	4
4	8	2	5	6	1	9	3	7
2	7	4	1	8	9	6	5	3
8	1	5	6	3	7	4	2	9
3	6	9	2	4	5	7	8	1

285

4	6	8	5	7	1	9	3	2
5	2	9	3	4	8	7	1	6
7	3	1	2	6	9	5	8	4
8	7	2	4	5	6	1	9	3
6	5	3	1	9	2	4	7	8
9	1	4	8	3	7	6	2	5
1	9	5	6	8	3	2	4	7
3	4	7	9	2	5	8	6	1
2	8	6	7	1	4	3	5	9

286

2	8	7	3	4	6	5	1	9
5	3	1	2	9	7	6	4	8
4	9	6	1	5	8	2	3	7
3	1	2	7	6	4	9	8	5
9	6	8	5	2	3	1	7	4
7	5	4	9	8	1	3	6	2
8	2	3	6	7	9	4	5	1
6	4	9	8	1	5	7	2	3
1	7	5	4	3	2	8	9	6

287

2	3	8	6	4	1	7	5	9
4	7	1	3	9	5	2	6	8
5	6	9	2	8	7	4	3	1
8	2	3	9	1	6	5	7	4
6	1	7	4	5	2	8	9	3
9	4	5	7	3	8	6	1	2
3	5	2	1	6	4	9	8	7
7	9	6	8	2	3	1	4	5
1	8	4	5	7	9	3	2	6

288

6	1	3	5	2	9	4	8	7
5	8	2	4	3	7	1	9	6
7	4	9	6	1	8	2	5	3
8	9	5	2	7	6	3	1	4
4	3	7	9	8	1	5	6	2
1	2	6	3	5	4	9	7	8
9	7	1	8	4	2	6	3	5
3	6	4	7	9	5	8	2	1
2	5	8	1	6	3	7	4	9